Best wishes!

Richard Steinheimer

THE ELECTRIC WAY ACROSS THE MOUNTAINS

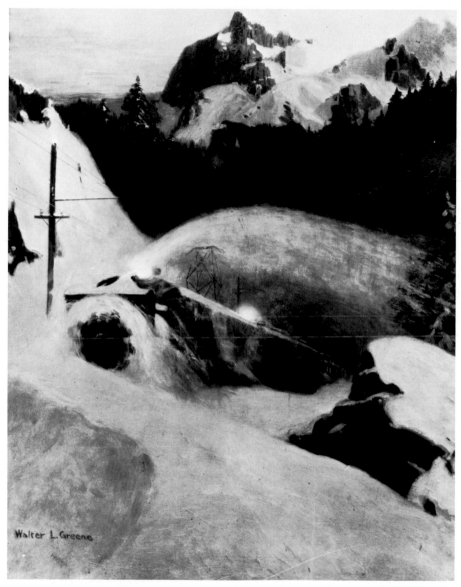

Walter L. Greene

General Electric

Books by Richard Steinheimer

BACKWOODS RAILROADS OF THE WEST
WESTERN TRAINS
THE ELECTRIC WAY ACROSS THE MOUNTAINS

THE ELECTRIC WAY ACROSS THE MOUNTAINS

STORIES OF THE MILWAUKEE ROAD ELECTRIFICATION

RICHARD STEINHEIMER

•

CARBARN PRESS

Tiburon, California

Dedicated to the men and women of the Milwaukee Electrification,

whose openness and delight with life have been an inspiration.

Richard Steinheimer 1979

Milwaukee enginemen, Avery, Idaho, 1974, Ted Benson

THE ELECTRIC WAY ACROSS THE MOUNTAINS

© 1980 Richard Steinheimer

Printed and bound in the United States of America.

Library of Congress Catalog Card No. 79-90763
I.S.B.N. 0-934406-00-6

First printing: January 1980

FRONT ENDPAPER
Milwaukee right-of-way east of Hyak, Washington, 1963.

CONTENTS

Rail bond, East Portal, Montana

Motorman's view from Bipolar in 1920's, General Electric

ACKNOWLEDGEMENTS

The photographers are due special thanks for making their works available for this book. Among them are: Ed Austin, Randy Austin, Ted Benson, Dr. Philip R. Hastings, John C. Illman, Arthur S. Jacobsen, Philip C. Johnson, Warren R. Magee, Warren M. Marcus, Walter C. Miller, Elizabeth Nixon, Ron V. Nixon, Wade J. Stevenson, Don Sims, Max Tschumi, Wilbur C. Whittaker, W.H. Wilkerson and Laurence Wylie.

Photographers like Benson, Johnson, Sims, Stevenson and Nixon are familiar names. But I would like to single out three less well known persons for special mention: Max Tschumi of Vancouver, B.C., whose pictures are among the finest ever done on the electrification; Noel T. Holley of Seattle and Arthur S. Jacobsen of Great Falls who were able to help the author get to the heart of stories about the electrification and its history.

The contributions of former employees of the Milwaukee Road have been invaluable. Their names include: the late Willard "Bill" Brautigam, who would have loved sipping a cocktail and looking at this book; Joe Brand, Alan R. Burns, George Frazier, Adam and LaVera Gratz, Don Goodsell, Robert Janin, Leo "Dude" Kemp, Bill Lintz, T. Barry Kirk, Norman Kistler, Jim Lowery, W.H. Merrill, Walter C. Miller, Dan O'Bannan, Roy E. Peterson, Jimmy Petersen, George "Blondie" Rainville, Harold Theriault, the late Laurence Wylie, and W.H. "Bill" Wilkerson.

Among others helping with pictures were: Tom Brown, A. Bruce Butler, Don Dietrich, Jeanne Engerman and Caroline Gallacci of the Washington State Historical Society, Ken Germann, Adam Gratz, George Horna, Freeman Hubbard, Ruth Larsen Lindow, Dr. G.A. Lintz, Warren M. Marcus, Keith and Dawn Newsom, Sandy Cannon, Dan Perkins, Harold Theriault, D.V. Thompson, W.H. Wilkerson and Warren Wing.

The heavyweights in terms of support include: Wallace W. Abbey, director of corporate communications for the Milwaukee Road and his assistant, Jim Scribbins, Communications Resources manager; John F. McDermott, manager of Marketing Communications for General Electric; and the late Everett L. DeGolyer Jr., founder of the DeGolyer Library at Southern Methodist University in Dallas.

The uncredited pictures in the book are the work of the author, most of which are included in the DeGolyer Library collection.

Warren M. Marcus, and his wife, Adrienne, were of particular help to the author in development of the insight necessary to approach this subject.

INTRODUCTION

I am very pleased to be able to bring to you *The Electric Way Across The Mountains,* a pictorial history of the 60-year life of the Chicago, Milwaukee, St. Paul & Pacific Railroad's electrification.

You'll see the camera artistry of several generations of master photographers, and meet some of the people from Washington, Idaho and Montana whose lives were part of this great adventure.

You will discover how the electrification, that was anticipated even before the Model T automobile, was able to keep swimming against the swift currents of technological change, and survive well into the Space Age.

Back in the year 1915, the Milwaukee Road's electric mainline west of Harlowton, Montana, was world famous. It became the prototype for similar high voltage direct current systems in Argentina, Brazil, Chile, France, India, Russia, Spain, Asia, and Africa.

This fame was no accident. The Milwaukee's wonderful publicity people staged dramatic "tug-of-wars," and other news events, to capture the attention of the world press. The Milwaukee Road showed the world a daring vision of the future for railroading.

Perhaps this book can lay to rest the idea the Milwaukee was not a heavy duty operation.

The record speaks for itself. In 1915 the new Mallet Compounds of other railroads could barely drag trains over mountain grades at seven or eight miles an hour, while having to stop to take water at nearly every water tank along the way.

At this same point in history, the Milwaukee was already operating multiple-unit locomotives with DC traction motors, and performance very similar to some of today's diesel-electric engines. In very cold weather, or in heavy snow, the Mallets were nearly incapable of moving even themselves, while the electrics gained performance, from the cooling of the electrical components. And, unlike those steam engines, the electrics never had to stop for water or fuel.

In fact, the electrics did not burn anything. Their power came from falling water, *White Coal,* if you will.

To top it all off, when the electrics went downhill with tonnage trains, their regeneration helped hold back the train and also kicked plenty of electricity back into the trolley wire.

On many days, Bob Williams or other Milwaukee Road substation operators would end their shifts with watt meters indicating they had taken more electric power out of the trolley wire than they had put into it!

In the pages of this book, you'll travel to the General Electric plant at Erie, Pennsylvania, in 1915, to see the first Milwaukee boxcab passenger engine meeting the light of day; probably the most powerful passenger locomotive in the world at that time. You'll see the two new classes of motive power which arrive in 1919, either one of which could qualify as the heaviest, and most powerful, single-unit passenger locomotive.

In addition, you will see the camera work of many lesser-known photographers, such as A.H. Armstrong, chairman of the General Electric Electrification Committee, who leaned out of his sleeping car vestibule on Pipestone Pass in 1915 to photograph a motive power conflict that would not be settled on other railroads for another three or four decades.

You will meet the Milwaukee's most famous engineer; and take a spectacular ride over St. Paul Pass with engineer Adam Gratz. Then you will experience the incredible violence of an icy winter night's ride over the same mountains.

Photographs of a memorable "race" between the *Olympian* and the *North Coast Limited*, on the eve of World War II, come to us from Ron V. Nixon, one of the great railroad photographers in the Northwest.

The interesting terrain through which the electrification operated is part of the book, too, from the rain forests of the Cascades to the deserts of Eastern Washington and the sparsely settled valleys and mountains of Montana.

You'll meet fireman Bill Merrill, who describes the delight of engineer Roy Cleveland and conductor Charlie Saint when they discover the Montana Power Company OWES THE RAILROAD $1.40 for the power used to haul the first electric freight train 38 miles across the Continental Divide hill. Bill also tells us about a dangerous night on the same hill, when five of his companions never live to see the dawn.

A dramatic newstory tells you about Ed Dulock, who takes his Bipolar over the 2.2 percent Saddle Mountains grade faster than anybody ever went before, to try to save the lives of his fellow workers.

The story is told, too, of Laurence Wylie, one of the greatest figures of the electrification, who when diesels threaten again designs an auxiliary controller to allow electric engineers to control diesel "boosters," but not the other way around.

The Milwaukee Road electrification was the most wonderful show in the world. It was a great adventure that many people shared.

I hope you enjoy the story.

Los Altos, California   Richard Steinheimer

August 18, 1979

THE EARLY YEARS

The Sunday walk of train order operators Kathy Ray and Vivian Smith, on a beautiful winter day at Bryson, Montana, is one of the most charming images to come down to us from the early days on the Pacific Extension of the Chicago, Milwaukee & St. Paul Railway. The Bitterroot Mountains wilderness, in which the ladies are walking, was crossed earlier by the rails of the Northern Pacific's Wallace branch (extreme right). The mountains still display the scars of the 1910 fire, which destroyed millions of acres of prime Idaho and Montana timber. The holocaust drove people, bears, deer and other wildlife together into the tunnels for safety; all temporarily united by fear.

The last spike on the Pacific Extension had been driven on May 14, 1909, 170 miles eastward at Gold Creek. This 1400-mile extension to Tacoma, Washington, from Mobridge, South Dakota, cost the railroad $233 million, a tremendous amount of money in those days. In retrospect, the line should never have been built. Traffic is proving to be light, with the Milwaukee making few inroads into the business of the entrenched Union Pacific, Northern Pacific and Great Northern railroads. The opening of the Panama Canal in 1914 only serves to dilute the already sparse freight business.

From President Albert J. Earling on down to the lowest level, Milwaukee management knows that something will have to be done to cut operating expenses and improve train operations.

That "something" is to evolve into the first long-distance electrification of a mainline railroad.

One hundred miles to the east, the steam powered *Columbian* passenger train pauses before the Milwaukee's magnificent new depot in Missoula, one of the first of many generations of trains destined to pass in front of this Montana landmark in the next 65 years.

Steam locomotives are still in charge of the Pacific Extension in this depot scene at Piedmont, Montana. The view toward the Continental Divide grade looks strangely vacant, without the forthcoming clutter of trolley poles and overhead wires; however, the first options for new power had already been signed by the Milwaukee. Across the Divide, the 2400-volt DC electrification of Milwaukee director John G. Ryan's Butte, Anaconda & Pacific Railway is setting new records for the hauling of ores from Butte Hill. The success of the BA&P in 1913 is the last assurance required by President Earling, and the rest of his board, that electrification of the Extension is the answer to their problems.

(Right) Prior to completing the electrification of the Rocky Mountain and Missoula Division mainlines, the Milwaukee was already operating a 4½-mile 1500-volt DC electric line in Great Falls, Montana. This small operation was initiated to comply with a local desire to remove steam engines from the city center.

Milwaukee Roa

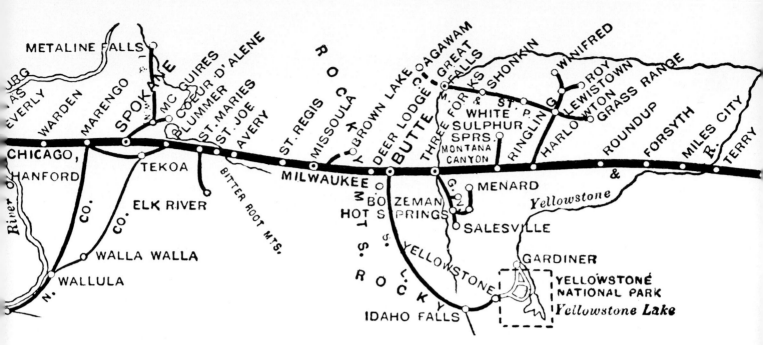

A 1916 map of the Pacific Extension trackage west of Miles City, Montana, shows the route of the 440-mile mainline electrified district that will reach from Harlowton, on the east, to Avery, Idaho, on the west.

Harlowton, a small cattle and farming town, was named for Richard A. Harlow, president of the Montana Railroad, the old "Jawbone" line, the Milwaukee predecessor in this area. Reputedly it was Harlow's "jawbone" that kept the Montana Railroad solvent for most of its years. The village of Avery was named for Avery Rockefeller, a member of the famous Standard Oil family, once associated with the Milwaukee Road management.

(Below) Two hundred miles up the branch line from Harlowton we see the trim little "substation in a room" at Falls Yard, source of the 1500-volt direct current used in the Great Falls operation. A scaled-down prototype for those substations planned for the mainline, it continues to operate until 1936 when a line change and internal combustion power obsoletes this Montana institution.

The advance men for an electrification technology that will spread all around the world pose modestly in front of Substation No. 4 at Eustis, Montana, early in 1915. Construction of the first stage of the system, between here and Deer Lodge, began in April 1914, under the direction of Reinier Beeuwkes, a brilliant young electrical engineer from The Netherlands. Eustis is located eight miles down the Missouri River from Three Forks, at the west end of Montana Canyon.

(Right) Construction gangs drill the holes in the rails for rail bonds at Butte yard. As a young line inspector, recently out of Montana State College, Laurence Wylie will ask why the cedar poles are not being creosoted before being placed into the ground. The youngster, who will become one of the most famous personages of the electrification, is told, "They'll last long enough; the anticipated life of this electrical system is 30 years."

The first section of 3000-volt trolley to be energized will be on the two percent grade east of the Continental Divide, near Butte. At Butte Yard, or possibly Three Forks, we see a trolley construction train at work, with the smoke-producing steam engine separated from the workmen by a convenient flatcar.

(Below) One of the 40-foot untreated Idaho Cedar trolley poles being installed by a crew using a GE gas-electric car. The total cost of the 440-mile electrification between Harlowton and Avery, including replacement of steam power, will be $12 million. In ten years it will be found that this investment has repaid itself twice, with interest.

General Electric's design for the electrification included assistance with financing of the $12 million system. GE had recently completed the successful 2400-volt Butte, Anaconda & Pacific installation, and was interested in creating an even larger demonstration of the merits of high-voltage direct current railroading. After the $233 million construction cost of the Pacific Extension, perhaps it was GE's financing offer which helped the Milwaukee directors to turn down the proposal from Westinghouse Electric Corporation. That proposal called for a 14,000-volt, 25-cycle, split-phase alternating current system similar to that completed in 1915 on a short stretch of Norfolk & Western Railroad mainline in West Virginia. —Author

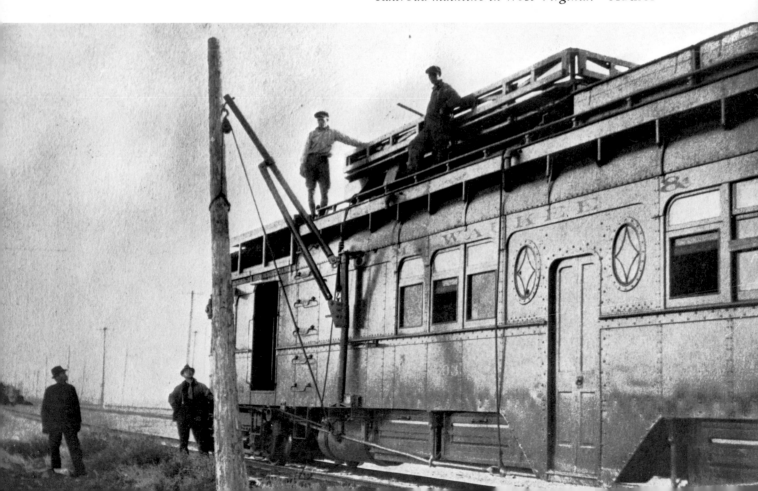

General Electric

(Left) Tower cars provide working platforms for the final alignment and tensioning of the twin 4/0 trolley contact wires and their network of supports. This photograph depicts a wire crew at work with hand tools and block and tackle. The twin contact wires (shown in silhouette, above) are hung from half-inch steel messenger wire by steel hangers, spaced so each 4/0 contact wire is supported alternately every 15 feet. After but a few years of operation, the Milwaukee will find that the addition of graphite grease to the pantograph contacts will virtually eliminate wearing of the trolley wire. **Harold Theriault Collection**

(Top) Substation No. 1 at Two Dot, 13 miles west of Harlowton, is in disarray as workmen assemble the two 2000-KW motor-generator sets. Less than 20 years later, on a very windy night, a transformer explosion will blow out the back of the substation, burning down the town's two bars, post office and fire station. The loss of the two watering holes is to be greatly lamented, and Two Dot will become the only substation on the system without an enclosed transformer room.

(Below) The very last segment of trolley to go into service will be through St. Paul Pass tunnel, across the Montana-Idaho state line, in the Bitterroot Mountains. Substation No. 13, at East Portal, will enter service in late 1916.

Milwaukee Road

THE MONSTERS OF ERIE

July 21, 1915, witnesses the first Milwaukee passenger motor, No. 10100, meeting the light of day outside GE's Erie Works. The 24 units which comprise this EP-1 class are visually distinguishable by the M-U socket hole above the cab door, the placement of the steam line, and the spring buffer above the coupler. Many years later, these same passenger units will continue to be identified by the round plate covering that M-U socket hole.

(Right) Noted here is the special passenger service equipment on the rear of unit 10105B; the components include steam boiler stack, double access ladders, modified buffer, and footboards. The GE235A traction motors utilized by the EP-1 motors are geared 71:29, for a top speed of 60 miles per hour. The one-hour rating of 3440 horsepower makes these 320-ton locomotive sets equal to a pair of General Motors GP9 diesels, still 40 years in the future.

This interesting scene shows at least ten Milwaukee Road boxcab units on the erecting floor of General Electric's Building 10, at Erie, Pennsylvania, on February 23, 1916. The only identifiable units seen from this elevated position are the third and fourth from the front, units from the 10102 and 10103 sets. The underframes for these motors were constructed under a sub-contract by the American Locomotive Company.

The Milwaukee locomotive order was placed in November 1914, and called for twelve, 60 miles per hour, two-unit passenger motors; and thirty, 30 miles per hour, two-unit freight motors. Though the passenger units were designed for single, as well as double unit operation, the freight units were semi-permanently coupled in pairs. With a continuous 3000-horsepower rating, these locomotives are the new monsters of electric railroading. . . General Electric's strongest answer to the then-new Mallet compound steam engines found on many American railroads. These electrics were the first high-voltage, direct-current, locomotives to use regenerative braking, an electro/mechanical system by which trains descending hills can control their speed and return electric current to the trolley system. In January 1917, the last of the Erie Monsters was on its way to Montana, for a career which would exceed its manufacturer's expectations several times over.

General Electric delivered the first boxcab set to the Milwaukee Road on September 25, 1915, in Chicago. The arrival of the 10200A&B set, class EF-1, touched off a classic advertising and sales promotion campaign, built around the "King of the Rails" theme. GE describes the 10200 as the largest electric locomotive in the world. Crowds estimated at over 10,000 people view the motors on display near Union Station. Though the Chicago, Milwaukee & St. Paul Railway is known as *The St. Paul Road* in Chicago, it is popularly called the *Milwaukee Road* out in Montana, where this new motor is headed.

(Right) Nearly 2000 miles to the west, at Avery, Idaho, a young locomotive fireman named Harold Theriault stands for his portrait after a dip in the St. Joe River. This Avery boy, who saw the first Pacific Extension surveyors walk down out of the North Fork, will grow to become one of the grand old men of the electrification.

This unusual publicity photograph depicts a nearly forgotten bit of history in the life of the Milwaukee's first mainline electric motors. The brand new 10200 stands at the head end of the westbound *Olympian* north of Chicago in late September, or early October, of 1915. The engine's pantograph reaches vainly for a 3000-volt trolley wire, still under construction 1500 miles to the west. The location of this unusual "action photo" on non-electrified trackage has been identified by the Milwaukee's engineering department as Forest Glen, Illinois, 10.2 miles north of the Windy City, on the mainline to Milwaukee.

(Below) The triumphant Western tour of No. 10200 includes a brief visit to Alberton, Montana, a division point west of Missoula. Though throngs of people admire the engine in the major cities of the Northwest, Harold Theriault's scrapbook records the 10200 as "The baby that put me on the tramp." The young fireman will be furloughed from the Milwaukee senority board at Avery in 1917, as the new electric power replaces the less efficient steam engines. Theriault will go railroading in Alaska for several years, before he will be called back to Milwaukee employment.

Two Photos— General Electric

The Baby that put me on the tramp.

(Above) The very first operation of a Milwaukee Road boxcab in the West is depicted in this rare photograph, taken in mid-October 1915, on the Butte, Anaconda & Pacific Railway. Shortly after arriving in Butte from Chicago, on its Western tour, No. 10200, with President Albert J. Earling's private car, undertakes a round trip to Durant beneath the 2400-volt BA&P overhead. Though the performance is diminished a bit by the low voltage, President Earling tells the press he is very pleased with the operation of his new electric locomotive.

The following month, the 10200 and 10201 will be tested on the BA&P to determine, in advance, the effectiveness of their regenerative braking. The feature was not incorporated into the BA&P engine fleet. After the successful conclusion of these tests, the Milwaukee motors will be assigned to helper service on the east side of the Pipestone Pass grade.

No. 10200 entered helper service in early November 1915, at Piedmont, while they still had steam engines pulling trains. We helped trains up to the summit at Donald, and over the pass to Janney, but not beyond because the wire wasn't energized. Walter R. Rowland was the first engineer to get paid for operating the 10200 in freight service, and I was his fireman.

The special with Earling on it was the second through train that they ran. The first was a test train from Piedmont to Butte, a freight with only local officials on it. They took 1250 tons up the two percent grade with the same motor that was in helper service. The trolley wire was up, but it wasn't energized past Butte because the substations were not completed.

When the train got over to Butte, they put 1750 tons behind the motor and came back. The grade from Butte to the summit, not being as long or steep as the grade out of Piedmont, allowed them a heavier haul on the trip back.

The motors had kilowatt-hour meters on them to tell how much power they used. The crew took a reading at Butte, at the top of the grade, and at Piedmont. The engineer, Roy Cleveland, and his conductor, Charlie Saint, announced that Montana Power Company owed the Milwaukee Road exactly $1.40 for that entire trip back from Butte! They had regenerated more current coming down the long grade into Piedmont than they had used to get up out of Butte!
—Retired fireman W.H. "Bill" Merrill

THE ELECTRIC WAY ACROSS THE MOUNTAINS

The great adventure that is the Milwaukee electrification has its formal beginning on the morning of November 30, 1915, in the cowboy country of Western Montana. In this photograph, by General Electric's A.H. Armstrong, we observe motor 10200 and its special train preparing to leave the yard at Three Forks for the first offical run over the mainline. A crowd has gathered to see this bit of history being made. At approximately 10:20 a.m. motorman Roy Cleveland, accompanied by fireman Billy Hart, pulls back the 32-point throttle and heads toward Eustis with caboose 0801 and President Earling's private car *Walworth*. At Eustis, the train will reverse direction and head back through Three Forks for the 70 mile run over Pipestone Pass to Butte. The hum of No. 10200's traction motors on the Continental Divide grade signals the beginning of the end for Milwaukee steam power on the high passes of Montana.

(Below) One week later, on December 8, President Earling and the board of directors stand at Janney substation to watch the 10201 and midtrain helper 10200 take a 3000-ton train up the

1.66 percent grade at 16 miles per hour, humbling the comparative efforts of three steam engines dragging 2000 tons over the same grade. As the electrics roll past the impressed directors, they demonstrate, as words cannot, that management's faith in electrification has been well placed. Soon thereafter, the directors approve plans for extension of the trolley system west from Deer Lodge, across the Missoula Division to Avery, Idaho.

Milwaukee Road

PIPESTONE PROPHESY

The life and death battles that will rage across the West in the 1950's, between locomotives driven by expanding steam and those driven by electric traction motors, had already been fought and won by electricity 40 years earlier on Pipestone Pass. Here, motor 10200, with steam boiler and freight gearing, is already showing its improvement over steam power with the *Olympian* in early December 1915. Hoary, as if with age, these beautiful A.H. Armstrong photographs capture one of those cold Montana afternoons when No. 15 requires an electric helper at Piedmont before heading into the snowy wilderness of the Rockies. Near Grace, Armstrong leans out of his *Olympian* sleeping car to take this incredible photo . . . a Pacific and a boxcab acting out the drama and sense of futility that people who love steam engines will feel many years later when the battles come to Sherman, Donner, Stampede, and other Western passes.

(Below) Passenger motor 10100 shows what high-speed, long-distance electric passenger service looks like in the state of Montana in 1916. The train is the eastbound *Olympian* in Silver Bow Canyon, west of Butte. Now, more than 60 years later, the leaders in long-distance electric railroad travel are the nations of Europe and Asia.

A11848-25

The little village of Roland, Idaho, steam helper town, is pictured during the Christmas season of 1916. Beyond the two-story depot is the west portal of St. Paul Pass tunnel. Soon the tunnel's electrical work will be finished, closing the last gap in the 440-mile network between Harlowton and Avery. Shortly after the first of the year, electric locomotives will begin running straight through and the little town of Roland will begin that decline from which there is no return.

(Right) Willard "Bill" Brautigam at Avery circa 1917, with his future father—in—law Frank Kroll. Brautigam came to Avery as an electrician, after grad-uation from the Uni-versity of Washington.

Mayna Brautigam Collection

We both got fired for it later, but two of us created a useful device for the GE boxcabs while I was working at Avery in the 1920's.

Frank MacAvoy, our traveling engineer, asked me one day if there wasn't some way to prevent the heavy slack actions at the top of the mountain as engineers put their motors into regeneration.

I thought about it quite a bit and a few weeks later took a trip with MacAvoy over the hill. It was a short train with no helper. When we got to the top, inside the Taft (St. Paul Pass) tunnel, we cut out the rear unit.

I went back into the electrical compartment of the lead unit while Frank sat at the throttle and kept juice in the traction motor fields. He watched his ammeter to see when armature current built up to the same 3000-volt level as the trolley.

When it got there, he yelled, and I manually threw a relay to put the motor into regeneration. It went in smoothly as could be, proving we could solve the regeneration problem with a balancing relay, to throw only when the two voltages were at the same level.

So, I went back and filed a patent for that new balancing relay. Of course, Ed Sears, the master mechanic, didn't hear anything about it until I'd already filed. He went through the roof. He got the officials to get people out from GE to devise a better system. But hard as they tried, they could not do it.

He got MacAvoy out of his traveling engineer's job and finally fired me. But the chief mechanical officer brought me to Tacoma where I stayed as chief electrician until it was safe to go back to the Rocky Mountain Division.

By that time the 'Brautigam Relay' was in everyday use. —Bill Brautigam

Though the term 'engineer' is the most common title for men operating the Milwaukee Road's electric locomotives, early train order forms and instruction manuals use the title 'Motorman.' —Author

According to the 1917 Special Instructions, the Staff Signal System is a crude form of automatic block, without sensors, for train detection. The Staff, actually, is a metal bar with cams. By inserting one of these devices into a relay box at a station, the crew is given authority to proceed onto the next section of track. Any other crew trying to remove another set of Staffs for the same district would be unable to do so, because of the protective interlocks. —Arthur S. Jacobsen

(Above) Not all operations over the Bitterroots are immediately converted to electricity, as demonstrated in this difficult moment when a steam rotary finds itself chewing up parts of the forest, as well as snow, in a slide below Falcon.

(Below) More typical of the new era is this scene at East Portal, where a single EF-1 motor, and steam rotary, are posed with its crew. The round hoop in the hand of motorman J. E. Pears holds the engine crew's half of the Staff, which conveys operating rights between this location and the next station. The Staff System will be used, in place of an automatic block signal system, on the Bitterroots grade until the early 1940's.

(Left) Another view of the *Olympian* in lonely Montana Canyon. This wild area is populated mainly by rattlesnakes, and a few very hardy ranchers.

(Above) Like other photographers, Asahel Curtis rides into Montana Canyon on a section car, where he is shown sitting with his gear. The negative is identified as, "Our Special In Montana Canyon."

OLYMPIAN ELEGANCE

Asahel Curtis, the Seattle photographer well known for his photographs of the Pacific Northwest, undertook a number of trips to Montana, with his 8x10 camera, for the ever-alert publicists of the Chicago, Milwaukee & St. Paul Railway. His journey on July 6, 1916, to the eastern portal of Eagle Nest tunnel in Montana Canyon (sometimes known as Sixteen Mile Canyon), results in a number of high quality pictures. Among them is this view of the all-steel *Olympian* behind motor 10102. . . a lasting portrait of *Olympian* elegance in the early days of the century. Passengers, looking out of their car windows, are still able to see portions of the old Montana Railroad right-of-way. This meandering low level route is covered over in most places by the new Milwaukee line.

The $12 million spent to electrify the 440 miles of Rocky Mountain and Missoula Division mainlines gives this revitalized railroad a capacity unimaginable with steam locomotion.

Westward up the valley of the Yellowstone River come the smoky coal burning steam engines, yielding at Harlowton to the power of White Coal. The big black EF-1 and EP-1 units hardly seem to strain with their loads until they reach the heavy grades, such as at Bruno, where a short stretch of 2 percent ruling grade causes freight trains, only, to take on helpers, or double the hill.

Then from the top of the Belt Mountains at Loweth, they begin the long descent to the Missouri River at Lombard, and roll westward to Three Forks on the Lewis and Clark Trail, before the easy running up the valley of the Jefferson to the foot of the Rockies at Piedmont. On over the mountains to Butte, and Deer Lodge, and down the valley of the Clark Fork to the St. Regis, and then over the Bitterroots to the forks of the St. Joe. Its Super Railroading, happening in one of the most sparsely settled regions of the United States, on a railroad that should never have been built.

But the great adventure is only beginning. The stage is now set for the next great expansion, one which will give the Milwaukee the longest electrified mainline in the world.

The Montana Canyon area has been struck by a number of heavy earthquakes, usually resulting in blockage of the rail line. There was a strong one in June 1925, and a very heavy one around 1933 or 1934. I was on a work train then, and recall them building a shoo-fly around the Deer Park tunnel, east of Lombard. No trains moved for days. Much rail was torn up in the canyon.

Another quake, in August 1959, did less damage in Three Forks but was very heavy in Helena. Northern Pacific trains then detoured over the Milwaukee.
—P.R. Roberts, engineer from 1911 to 1962

THE MIDDLE PERIOD

The unusual, new electric locomotives under construction at GE's Erie plant, are symbols of the new era of expansion coming to the Milwaukee Road electrification in 1919. This era we call The Middle Period, which begins with the Roaring Twenties and ends 30 years later in the technological uncertainties at the end of World War II.

These new 1–B+D+D+B–1 EP-2 class Bipolar locomotives will become famous in the 1920's, the symbol of what railroading is going to become in that never-never period "just around the corner." The Chicago, Milwaukee & St. Paul Railway is beginning its last great expansion of electric operations. First came the conquering of the Belts, Rockies and Bitterroots. Now the technology that worked so wonderfully across those mountains, is going to be extended over the Saddles and Cascades.

(Below) This rare photograph, taken on April 9, 1919, shows the erection floor of Shop 10 with seven additional cab sections under construction. Can the engineers at General Electric forsee the fame and popularity which will be achieved by this small order of five locomotives? **General Electric**

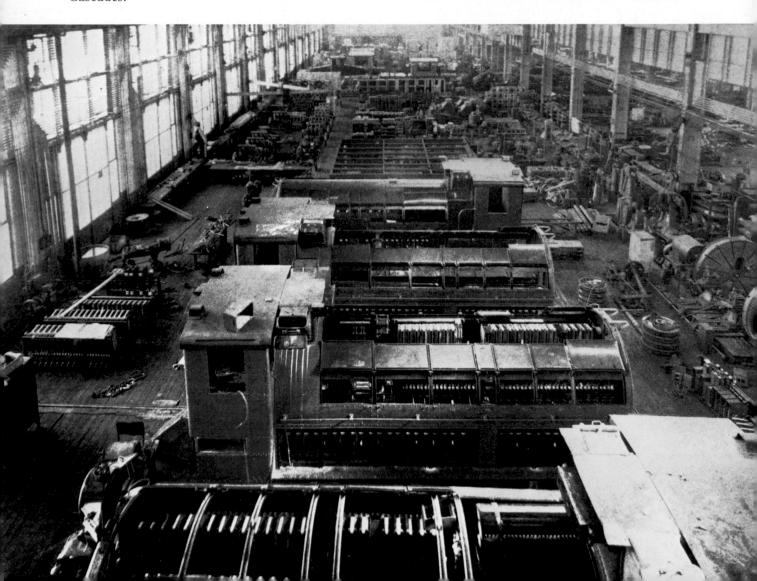

One of the proudest days in the life of Albert J. Earling, the Milwaukee Road telegrapher who rose to become president, comes on March 5, 1920, when a special train is run for members of the press, from Tacoma to Cle Elum, behind Bipolar 10254. On this trip, commemorating the opening of the 207-mile Coast electrification, Earling sees the near culmination of his dream at the turn-of-the-century which envisioned electric operation of the Pacific Extension. The man with the foresight to obtain powerhouse sites during construction of the line to Tacoma, has lived to see much of his vision become reality.

(Above) The occasion of that historic journey warrants a photo stop for members of the press near Easton, Washington. Bipolar 10254 displays a bit of a problem with the oil-fired train heat boiler, or a reaction to the chill air, as it poses for the camera of Asahel Curtis. Though today is the formal opening of the new electrified district, EF-1 freight motors have already been in operation for several months on the Cascade and Saddle mountain grades.

(Below) A classic portrait of Milwaukee Road management, posing proudly in front of the Cle Elum substation, with President Earling in the center. At the far right, a newsman gets the actual facts from a staff aide.

The $8,600,000 net cost of the Coast Division electrification shows one of the effects of the inflationary spiral caused by World War I. The net cost five years earlier for the installation in Idaho and Montana was $12 million, for a system more than twice the length.

(Above) Illustrating the high standard of design found within the new system, is the motor-generator room at the Cedar Falls substation. Two 2000-KW m-g sets are in place, and there is a provision for a third set should it be needed. Generally speaking, Coast substations are of slightly lower generating capacity than their Montana counterparts, but spaced closer together. Eight substations, of 30,000-KW total capacity, serve 207 miles of Pacific line, compared with 14 substations of 60,000-KW capacity for the Montana Division's 440 route miles.

(Below) The main electrical switchboard at Tacoma controls both AC and DC circuits, and is placed at the far side of the m-g room across from the operator's office. Coast substations, like those in Idaho and Montana, receive their 100,000-volt AC current from commercial utility sources. A current limiting system is used for a short time in this period to limit peak demands for power. It soon is eliminated when it becomes apparent that the Milwaukee's power requirements are not significant in relation to the total demand for power.

Among the most important trains operated by American railroads in the 1920's,
are the special Silk Trains transporting live
silk worms, in their precious cocoons, to
eastern markets. With 650 miles of electrical operation, the Milwaukee is a favorite
routing of the shippers.

The Milwaukee docks, adjacent to Tide
Flats yard in Tacoma, are favorite entry
points for the silk worms, and for the trans-
loading to ships of agricultural products
from the farm areas of the Northwest.

(Below) With its load of silk worms
aboard, Bipolar 10254 heads east through
Black River Junction, Washington. The 15-
car train is valued at $4.8 million, an astro-
nomical amount of money in the 1920's.
The worms travel in heated cars at better
than passenger train speeds, to assure their
arriving on the East Coast before they die,
or eat their way out of their silken cocoons;
either of which will ruin the silk.

BIPOLAR POWER

The Milwaukee Road was the last transcontinental railroad to reach the Puget Sound, and, therefore, had the most difficult job of soliciting business. Thus, on February 22, 1920, at Kent, Washington, the railroad graphically demonstrates the power potential of its new 260-ton Bipolar locomotives by having one of them take on, and humble, a large modern steam engine not unlike those of its competitors. Here, the crewmen of No. 10254 stand aggressively near their charge, barely tolerating the reporter attempting to record the story for the Seattle *Post-Intelligencer,* or other newspaper.

The crewmen of the ten-year-old 2-6-6-2 Mallet Compound steam locomotive stand relaxed and philosophical before engaging in the shoving contest that they will lose. No. 9520 has a total weight slightly greater than its Bipolar challenger, but exerts considerably less tractive effort. In cold winter weather, steam engines lose 20 to 30 percent of their pulling power, while electrics gain efficiency from lower temperatures.

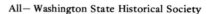

At first the steamer seems to have its way, with smoke billowing in the nippy February air. But as the throttle of the electric is opened, the protesting 2-6-6-2 is stopped in its tracks and then shoved backwards, past the army of press photographers and on-lookers. The railroad will go into receivership in 1925; but the point has been made. The Milwaukee has joined, on a better-than-even-standing, the other major railroad operations of the Northwest.

The brick building behind the contestants has been identified as a substation for the Puget Sound Electric Railway, confirming this location as being near the Milwaukee's Kent depot.

Because of the publicity attendant to the Milwaukee's new electric engines in the 1920 period, "Bipolar" becomes a household word along the shores of Puget Sound. There are never to be more than five Bipolars, yet they become a part of the fabric of everyday life in the Pacific Northwest, and an integral part of the business and travel scene around Seattle and Tacoma for more than three decades. To the man on the street, they are an institution unique to the Northwest, a touch of the future that someday will spread out from Washington state to modernize the railroads of the rest of the world.

One of the main contributors to this image is Asahel Curtis, a Seattle commercial photographer. Curtis records wonderful scenes, such as motor No. 10254 hauling the *Olympian*

past Humpback Mountain in the Cascades. The bundled-up passengers riding the open end observation car of that fine train may be chilled, but they are at least free from the soot and sparks associated with the steam-powered competitors of the Milwaukee.

(Left) Blending with these images are other Curtis pictures, such as that of the Great White Fleet visiting Seattle in the period before the First World War.

(Right) Another Curtis image depicts the titanic struggle on Change Creek trestle, in the Cascades, of a pair of Milwaukee steam engines with Bipolar 10253. This raw display of power is no doubt planned to catch the eye of rail-roaders on several Eastern roads, where new electric locomotive orders are presently under consideration.

Milwaukee Road— R. Janin Collection

THE MIGHTY QUILLS

Though the Bipolars are destined to become the Milwaukee's most famous locomotives, there are ten Baldwin-Westinghouse EP-3 class Quill-drive motors delivered in the same 1919-20 period of even more extraordinary power and size.

All— Milwaukee Road

(Above) When first delivered, motors like the No. 10300 weigh approximately 283 tons; but broken frames soon develop from the demands of the Milwaukee's steep grades and ten degree curves and the entire order is sent back to Baldwin to have the faults corrected.

(Right) Back from rebuilding, the giant motors now weigh nearly 310 tons and stand over 17 feet in height. Number 10302, on an eastbound consist near Falcon, has a one-hour rating of 4200 horsepower. The continuous rating is 3200 horsepower. The engines are 88 feet, 7 inches in length, and almost twice the weight and power of "similar" New Haven electric locomotives on the East Coast.

(Upper Right) The January 2, 1921, timetable shows the times of passage for the Milwaukee's two premier trains, something more relevant to the women primping in the lounge of the *Olympian* than the technical details of the new locomotives.

They were big and fast, and I think the smoothest riding electric locomotive of them all. They had more pickup than the Bipolars, which, with just two field poles and the axle-mounted armatures moving up and down with the wheels, weren't particularly efficient. But they were not as rugged in design. Even after they went back to the factory for rebuilding, we always were having to re-weld the frames.

They let me put a little more lateral movement into the center driving axles, but the flange wear problem was never really solved. These Westinghouse motors were operating around 10-degree curves on one of the most difficult mountain railroads in the country, and the quill drive just wasn't tough enough. The drivers were larger than necessary, too.

They used a generator situated on each front truck to excite the fields for regeneration. The Bipolars were set up so that four of the axles provided the field current for the remaining eight. Both systems worked pretty well. —Bill Brautigam, roundhouse foreman at Deer Lodge in 1924.

No. 15—The Olympian.
Chicago-Miles City-Butte-Spokane-Seattle-Tacoma.

	Example	Daily	(See tables 1 to 5).
Lv Chicago (Central Time)....	(Sun)	10.15 PM	
Lv Milwaukee..............	(Mon)	12.35 AM	*Observation Club Car.*
Ar St. Paul................	"	10.40 AM	Chicago to Seattle-Tacoma.
Lv St. Paul................	"	10.56 AM	*Parlor Car.*
Ar Minneapolis.............	"	11.30 AM	Spokane to Seattle-Tacoma.
Lv Minneapolis.............	"	11.45 AM	*Standard Sleeping Cars.*
Lv Aberdeen...............	"	8.45 PM	Chicago to Seattle-Tacoma.
Ar Mobridge...............	"	11.40 PM	Chicago to Spokane.
Lv Mobridge (Mount. Time)..	"	10.50 PM	Chicago to Minneapolis.
Ar Miles City.............	(Tues)	8.10 AM	□Milwaukee to Minneapolis.
Ar Harlowton.............	"	2.50 PM	
Ar Three Forks............	"	6.45 PM	*Tourist Sleeping Cars.*
Ar Butte..................	"	9.25 PM	Chicago to Seattle-Tacoma.
Ar Deer Lodge.............	"	10.40 PM	*Dining Car.*
Ar Missoula...............	(Wed)	12.51 AM	Chicago to Seattle-Tacoma.
Lv Avery.................	"	5.35 AM	(A la carte dinner).
Lv Avery ....(Pacific Time).	"	4.45 AM	
Ar Spokane...............	"	9.00 AM	*Coaches.*
Ar Seattle................	"	8.15 PM	Chicago to Seattle-Tacoma.
Ar Tacoma................	"	9.55 PM	

No. 17—The Columbian.
Chicago-Miles City-Butte-Spokane-Seattle-Tacoma.

	Example	Daily	(See tables 1 to 5).
Lv Chicago (Central Time)....	(Sun)	8.15 AM	
Lv Milwaukee..............	"	10.35 AM	
Ar St. Paul................	"	9.15 PM	
Lv St. Paul................	"	9.25 PM	*Standard Sleeping Cars.*
Ar Minneapolis.............	"	10.00 PM	Chicago to Seattle-Tacoma.
Lv Minneapolis.............	"	10.15 PM	St. Paul to Marmarth.
Lv Aberdeen...............	(Mon)	7.10 AM	⊙St. Paul to Aberdeen.
Ar Mobridge...............	"	10.15 AM	□Spokane to Seattle-Tacoma.
Ar Marmarth..............	"	4.50 PM	
Ar Miles City.............	"	8.55 PM	*Tourist Sleeping Cars.*
Ar Harlowton.............	(Tues)	4.45 AM	Chicago to Seattle-Tacoma.
Ar Three Forks............	"	8.50 AM	
Ar Butte..................	"	11.35 AM	*Parlor Car.*
Ar Deer Lodge.............	"	12.50 PM	Chicago to Minneapolis.
Ar Missoula...............	"	3.06 PM	
Ar Avery.................	"	7.45 PM	*Dining Car.*
Lv Avery ....(Pacific Time)..	"	6.55 PM	Chicago to Seattle-Tacoma.
Ar Spokane...............	"	11.30 PM	
Ar Seattle................	(Wed)	11.45 AM	*Coaches.*
Ar Tacoma................	"	1.35 PM	Chicago to Seattle-Tacoma.

Milwaukee Road— R. Janin Collection

THE LOVELY MARY GARDEN

One of the most famous celebrities of the 1920's is opera singer Mary Garden. Millions admired her, both for her beauty and for her singing abilities. At least once, while traveling with the Chicago Opera Company on the electrification, she is greeted by snowslides in the Bitterroots. In the spring of 1923 or 1924, the exact date being lost to time, Miss Garden is riding on the second of two trains carrying her troupe. As her train approaches Drexel, a huge avalanche blocks its progress. Also on board is Asahel Curtis, the photographer employed most by the Milwaukee Road.

While everyone waits for arrival of the rotary snow plow, Curtis passes his time by snapping photos of the troupe. In this superb photograph, Miss Garden is shown sitting in the engineer's seat of motor 10302, while her fellow performers are draped across the front of the engine. All are dressed in heavy clothing for this spring day in the Bitterroots. One can imagine the serious cigar-smoking gentleman at the right to be the booking agent for the troupe, upset over the delay. When the double-ended rotary set arrives from Avery, Curtis shoots the less fashionably dressed crewmen.

Walter C. Miller, retired conductor from Missoula, gives us his personal account of that exciting day:

On or about March 4, 1924, I was called as a brakeman on No. 263 out of Alberton with conductor John Sandberg and engineer Bill Milligan.

Our crew reported for work about 8:00 a.m. and, while we were waiting, the westbound **Olympian** *passed without stopping, about 5 hours late.*

We got going at about 9:30 a.m. and got as far as Tarkio, when the substation operator stopped us. After a long delay, we were instructed by Superintendent J.P. Phelan to take our engine and caboose to St. Regis.

Number 15 had been running late because of having to wait at Butte for the end of the performance given by the Mary Garden Opera Company, before the three sleepers and one baggage car at the rear of the train could be loaded. The famous singer and her company were on the way to an engagement in Spokane the following night.

Train No. 15 would have arrived in Spokane at about 2:00 p.m. There was a warm sun out, shining on the heavy snow pack. The whole countryside was beautiful and I often thought that the lovely Miss Garden was drinking in all this scenery.

At Foraker her train was moving rapidly, making up lost time, when suddenly the trolley went dead. The train rolled to a stop near the west switch, just in time!

A huge avalanche had fallen just 300 yards ahead of the train, carrying down trees, rocks and dirt. It was over 100 feet high and 400 feet long. The carrying away of the trolley had saved the train!

After several hours delay, the train was backed to St. Regis and delivered to the Northern Pacific for a detoured run to Spokane. The performance had to be cancelled and the whole country was concerned because of the close call of nearly having her train buried by the avalanche. We men of the rails thank our Heavenly Father for His protection.

The slide was finally cleared after about six days and nights of dynamiting and digging. Crews were fed and rested in two sleeping cars and a dining car at Haugan. We played a good role in the work.

To this day, railroad men point to the spot and talk about the near disaster. It is now known as the Mary Garden Slide.

—Walter C. Miller, retired conductor

Mrs. Vey Cornwall Collection

SKELETON CREW

E. S. DELLINGER

Railroad Magazine

Getting Elected to the Legislature Didn't Help—Harry Wardlow Had to Almost Break His Neck to Get the Full-Crew Law Enacted

A BRAND new juice jack was snaking a mile of freight cars west through the Northern Rockies. Harry Wardlow, the division's young electrical expert was at the controls. In his capacity as traveling engineer, he was out to test the performance of the E-1301 on her maiden trip over the Copper Mountain run.

Wardlow had taken the controls from his twin brother Dave an hour ago. Ruddy-faced, sandy-haired Dave had unceremoniously yanked their kid brother, Jack, out of the brakeman's seat and sitting stiff-necked and hot in the head, was now watching a cloud of elsan feathers with pink lightning shimmering at its edges over the Continental Divide.

94   95

DANGER AT PIEDMONT!

In February 1953, a story by railroad writer E.S. Dellinger appears in *Railroad Magazine,* one of the few fiction pieces written about mainline electric railroading. To a large degree, the story parallels events of the night of September 30, 1920, on the Continental Divide hill. W.H. "Bill" Merrill was there and tells us about the dangers of that beautiful moonlit night.

We were on a 96 car westbound freight train at Piedmont, made up mostly of old gravel cars with brakes that didn't work very well, and not holding their air pressure. Our helper motor was cut in about 35 cars from the head end. Conductor Lyons wanted to stay for a pair of meets with eastbound trains, but the dispatcher ordered us out. So up the grade we went.

Back in the helper, we only had 35 pounds of air instead of 90 pounds when we took the siding at Vendome, eight and one-half miles up the two percent grade. This siding only held 85 cars, so we had to saw by the first train, an eastbound freight. We had pulled forward through the siding to let him past our caboose. In backing down again to get ready for No. 18, a drawbar pulled out about five cars behind our helper.

I got out to help the brakeman put in a new drawbar, but the rear of the train started rolling. We tried to set some handbrakes as fast as we could, but by the time we looked at the ground it was going pretty fast. We both unloaded. Our conductor notified the operator at Piedmont of the runaway. An engineer, waiting in the depot for No. 18, ran out and jumped onto a motor to clear the mainline. The freight that had passed us was cutting out its helper there. Though the conductor rarely came

Piedmont Wreck C.M. and SP

out of his caboose, he happened to see the jiggling marker lights rushing down the mountain toward his train. The next thing he knew, when he became conscious again, he was down the right of way on the other side of a barbed wire fence. He had a torn glove but no idea how he got there.

As the rear of our runaway train smashed into the stopped train, an insulator from the trolley system flew off through the air and killed the engineer trying to clear the mainline. Five men, including an off duty employee, were riding an old water car on our train. Only one survived. Our rear brakeman rode the train down the hill and was seriously injured.

Since we'd left Three Forks without an air test, and the brakeman hadn't inspected our train, the government held our crew equally responsible with the company. That wreck was the biggest thing I remember happening.

THE
MOST FAMOUS
ENGINEER

On July 2, 1923, Warren G. Harding, President of the United States of America, becomes the most famous personage to fall under the spell of the Milwaukee electrification. On his way to a hunting trip in Alaska, Harding takes the throttle of motor 10305 on his own special train, at Sappington, Montana, and stays with the engine crew most of the rest of the way to Avery. "This is the most delightful ride I have even known in my life," he tells the press. He said "he drank in inspiration from riding the train down the 20 miles (into Avery) in regeneration, storing up energy sufficient to pull another train up-grade." Special plaques

commemorating this noble trip were attached to the locomotive beneath the cab windows, which the engine carried for the remainder of its career.

Sadly, the Milwaukee Road lost its most famous engineer a month after the ride, when the President took ill and died in San Francisco.

(Below) Less unusual is the operation of the important Silk Trains over the same route. In this classic 1926 view, we note Westinghouse motor 10306 pausing briefly on the 1.66 percent grade near Falcon, for the camera of Asahel Curtis. In a moment the 10306 will be on its way to St. Paul Pass, highballing the valuable little worms eastward.

Ron V. Nixon Collection

THE EXOTIC EXPERIMENT

Continued frame and flange-wear problems with the big Westinghouse motors in the 1920's leads to the creation of the Milwaukee's most rare, and exotic, electric locomotive. So brief is the life of this configuration that many railroaders will dispute its existence.

Strengthening of the Quill frames was at least partly successful, but attempts to correct the heavy wearing of driver tires and flanges on the ten degree mountain curves had failed. Therefore, at some point in the 1920's, motor 10301 is picked for an experiment to determine if performance can be improved by dividing the locomotive frame and superstructure into two units. The placing of two additional axles creates a 2-C-2+2-C-2 wheel arrangement; Hudsons back-to-back. The work apparently is done at Baldwin, where the frame strengthening took place.

(Above) This rare side view of the locomotive illustrates the division of the cab structure.

(Right) A beautiful June morning in 1926, in Missoula, finds No. 10301 arriving in its two-unit configuration with the eastbound *Olympian*. Next year the 10301 will be enroute to the Coast Division to assist the Bipolars, and to help tout the new *Olympian* equipment which will go into service in August 1927.

(Below) Official drawings of the two versions of the EP-3 class engines.

At some point in the late 1920's, the 10301 will be returned to Baldwin for reconversion to the standard configuration, thereby ending the brief life of this exotic experiment.

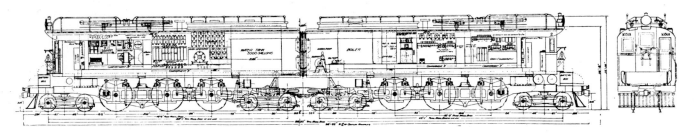

Milwaukee Road

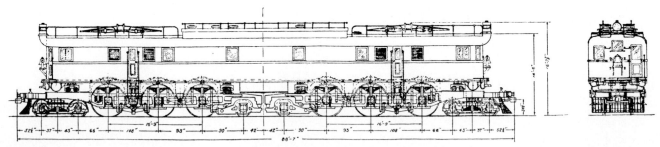

Until the trolley is completed into Seattle, on July 5, 1927, this 2-6-2 Prairie steamer has the job of shuttling passenger trains back and forth between Black River Junction and Seattle. Since there is no wye at Union Station, No. 5554 has been equipped with a back-up pilot on its tender, for the reverse movements to Black River.

(Below) While the little 2-6-2 is bringing the passenger trains to Seattle and return, mainline electric power like Bipolar 10253 waits patiently at the junction.

Two Photos— Warren Wing Collection

THE MAYOR RUNS A BIPOLAR

By 1920, electrification of the Coast Division had been completed, but the wires did not come to Seattle. An early cost study had indicated that it would be cheaper to continue hauling passengers and freight into Seattle with steam. Seattle and Tacoma were competing deep water ports on the Puget Sound. In those times, Tacoma was often considered more important. When the trolley wires got to Black River Junction, they only headed southward, down the fertile Kent Valley, to Tacoma's Tide Flats yard.

After the electrification had been in place for several years, experience showed that steam service to Seattle meant a loss rather than a saving. Steam engines were sitting idle between trains at Seattle and electrics were doing the same thing at Black River Junction.

A new study was initiated in 1925 by Reinier Beeuwkes, chief electrical engineer, to bring wires into Union Station and into the small freight yard at Van Asselt. Approval to do the work was granted in the fall of 1926. The Pacific Coast Railroad owned the tracks as far as Argo, and the Union Pacific owned them from there to the depot. These railroads offered no objections to expansion of the electrification.

The ten-mile route from Black River to Seattle was double-tracked, but the Milwaukee's usual system of guyed poles and span wires could not be used. There would be too much interference with other trackage and sidings. Beeuwkes chose double-armed poles, placed between the two mainline tracks, as the solution to this problem. Milwaukee right-of-way crews went to work moving one of the mainlines away from the centerline, and widening bridges, to provide clearance for the poles between the tracks. Steel poles were used near Union Station and on the sharper curves, for aesthetic purposes and to hold the load without the utilization of guy wires.

As the trolley was installed, it turned a bright copper-oxide green. Messenger wires and hangers were bronze instead of steel, because hot, corrosive steam locomotive exhaust gases had been rusting the galvanized fittings used on other areas of the Milwaukee electrification. The combination of Union Pacific steam trains, salt air from the Puget Sound, and Washington rainfall, was seen as sufficient incentive to use corrosion-resistant overhead.

On July 5, 1927, the Milwaukee Road inaugurated its last significant addition to the electrification. At 9:00 a.m. a special train filled with dignitaries and the press heads for Black River Junction. Among the passengers on this steam train are H.E. Byram, receiver and president; H.B. Earling, vice president; Beeuwkes; and Bertha Landes, the mayor of Seattle.

(Above) When the train reaches Black River, the steam engine is taken off. Its replacement is electric motor 10252, a Bipolar. Mayor Landes, assisted by engineer G.A. Bankson, takes the throttle for the trip back to Seattle. She wears a striped engineer's cap as she notches out the throttle and blows for the crossings.

*In the gaudy newspaperese of the 1920's, the Seattle **Post-Intelligencer** describes the train's arrival:* 'A great black thing of power with a string of yellow coaches like a kite tail behind, the first great electric monster of the Chicago, Milwaukee & St. Paul Railroad to pull into Seattle, making this the terminal of the longest electrified railroad in the world.' —Noel T. Holley

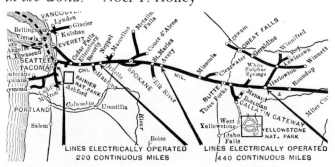

LINES ELECTRICALLY OPERATED 220 CONTINUOUS MILES   LINES ELECTRICALLY OPERATED 440 CONTINUOUS MILES

Elizabeth Nixon

Among Nixon's mentors in photography is his mother, Elizabeth Nixon. While in Three Forks, in the summer of 1931, she captures on film the steam-powered Gallatin Gateway connection to Yellowstone Park. The little 4-6-0 has backed its train onto the rear of the westbound *Olympian*, to allow direct transfer of first class passengers headed for Bozeman, and the wilds of Yellowstone.

MEETING OF THE **COLUMBIANS**

The dramatic meeting of the east and westbound *Columbian* passenger trains, in November 1928, at Willow Creek, is captured by a young Bozeman high school student, Ron V. Nixon. Westinghouse motor 10305, on the eastbound consist, carries a plaque just behind the cab commemorating the July 1923 ride of President Harding from nearby Sappington to Avery. Flying snow and the chilly November air have cleared the rear platform of the westbound's observation car, where, in the shadows, a brakeman waves back to the engineer of "The Harding Engine." In later years, Ron V. Nixon will become one of the great photographers of the Northwest and pursue a long career in communications with the Northern Pacific Railroad.

The **Quill** *nickname given to Baldwin-Westinghouse motors comes from the hollow 15-inch 'quill' tube surrounding each drive axle. The tube takes torque from the twin-armature traction motor and transmits it to the spokes of the drive wheels. Since the axle rides free, and the motor and quill are suspended from the carbody, there is little unsprung weight, giving the engines an excellent ride, despite the huge 68-inch drivers.*
—Author

47

ROUGH TRACK AHEAD

One wonders if Asahel Curtis can anticipate the brink of disaster upon which the world is poised when he takes this classic picture of the eastbound *Columbian*, behind motor 10300, on No Name trestle, in Loop Creek Canyon above Avery. The date: October 1929. This is the month of the crash on Wall Street, where $15 billion in paper assets will "evaporate" by the end of the year.

(Below) The hard times are not the fault of the electrification, but we see a Westinghouse motor joining in the general suffering by hitting a slide in the Bitterroots. Wrecker X10 will soon have the line cleared and the train on its way.

A 1925 report shows the electrification had already returned a net profit of $12.4 million by 1924. The first electrified district returned 21 percent per year on investment, less bond interest. In 1923, 59 electric locomotives were doing the work of 167 steam engines. —Author

(Above) This derailment of a pair of boxcab units, along the North Fork of the St. Joe River, is one of the exciting highlights of life in the Bitterroots in the Roaring Twenties. It also inspired a name for the little creek nearby, forever after to be known as Motor Creek. It is all part of the perilous Twenties for the Milwaukee, dangerously overcapitalized by the costs of the Pacific Extension. In a style of operation later to become popular with government, the original estimate for the Extension of $60 million was met by actual costs of nearly $260 million.

(Below) The three grim looking gentlemen surveying the property in 1925 are among the court appointed receivers for the Milwaukee, which was declared bankrupt in March of that year. Identifiable figures are Harry E. Byram, center, the former president, and Henry A. Scandrett, right, about to become president of the successor company, the Chicago, Milwaukee, St. Paul & Pacific Railroad. But by 1935, even the reorganized company will be bankrupt.

I came to Avery shortly after the wire was completed to that remote little division point along the St. Joe River. In addition to my electrician's duties, I set up a generator in the river and sold power to the hotel and other people. I charged $1 a month for the first outlet and $.50 for the next.

Then a woman sold me some AAA leghorn chickens that weren't laying. The sun shone only a few hours a day in winter, so I put them up on the hill by the roundhouse and Hoghead Gulch. I ran a light up there, timed to go on before dawn.

The guys at the roundhouse coming off work used to see the light in the chickenhouse and kid, 'Yep, Brautigam's working his chickens overtime again tonight!' But I always got an egg a day from those chickens. —Bill Brautigam

49

NEW ECONOMIES

The worsening of business conditions in the early 1930's brings a number of new economies and changes. The little "ES-01 Class" shop switcher has been built from a truck of the scrapped Gallatin Valley Electric Railway car number 3.

An operational change involves the use of Westinghouse passenger motors in fast freight service. We see motor 10307 eastbound on the Continental Divide grade, above Butte, in 1933. Their air pumps limit them to a maximum 50 car train.

(Below) A major economy comes from the creation, in 1932, of twelve new EF-2 class three-unit freight motors, such as No. 10503, seen in the fall of 1933 at Willow Creek. Later in the 1930's, shopmen will cut away the pony trucks and part of the cab structure of the center units, to create the first "bob-tail" center units, for the new EF-3 class.

All— Ron V. Nixon

I remember when I came to Avery, and worked under live trolley again, how careful people had to be. I was on the top of the boiler of an S-3 steamer one day with an ICC man. He forgot. . . and started to stand up. I grabbed him. 'You're two seconds away from electrocuting us!', I told him.

If people got shocked, we were supposed to use the Pullmotor to revive them. But in practice, we saw that you had to attach a sharp metal clamp to the person's tongue, to keep them from accidentally swallowing it.

Well, one day, one of our Japanese foremen, Taketa, was lifting a live steam pipe out of the tank of a tender. It hit the trolley and the 3000 volts knocked him off the tender onto the ground. The pipe took most of the current, so Taketa was becoming conscious about the time Earl Walters came running with the Pullmotor.

Taketa saw him coming, and thinking about that painful tongue clamp, staggered to his feet and took off running. So there we were. . . Taketa running away. . . with Earl chasing him as fast as he could run with the Pullmotor!

We laughed until tears came. But that Taketa, he had class. —Roy E. Peterson, roundhouse foreman

At one time my wife, LaVera, and I were sitting in the beanery at Avery and an old engineer came in off a passenger train and sat down with us.

It turned out he'd been having problems with the balancing relay on his Westinghouse motor coming down the hill into town. He'd gone on and explained what a problem the whole thing was, when LaVera cut in and said, 'Why didn't you put in a jumper from the N-wire to the P-wire?'

There was a long silence, and then the old hogger asked her, 'How did you know THAT?'

She told him, 'I read it so many times with Adam when he was studying the books for promotion to engineer, who could forget it?'

It was true, LaVera was as much a part of my passing the tests on those locomotives as I was. Like other wives, I guess, she had to sit for hours asking questions from the books. —Adam Gratz

AVERY MISHAP

(Above) In 1933, the massive flooding of the St. Joe River, as in this view of Avery yard under water, causes one of the few serious passenger train derailments and sets the stage for a maddening derailment ten years later.

Torrential rains were falling in the Bitterroots on December 23, as the westbound *Columbian* was beginning its descent to Avery under the control of engineer A.E. Blundell, one of the heroes of the 1910 fire. At Stetson, Blundell seemed to have the mountain whipped. But just inside the Avery yard limits, with a block signal showing green into the depot, Blundell suddenly realized that on this trip he had lost his continuing battle with the mountain. With brakes in the "big hole," No. 10303 slid out onto a trestle undermined by the cascading flood waters, and toppled off into the North Fork.

Blundell, always the hero, held his trapped fireman's head above water until rescuers could arrive on the scene. Now it will be weeks before a track can be laid down to the wrecked motor so it can be raised. Back on the rails, the engine will be taken to Deer Lodge and stored behind the roundhouse. In 1939 it tentatively will be renumbered E19.

Around September 15, 1942, shopmen at Deer Lodge will begin to scrap the inactive old motor, to contribute metal to the war effort. But as a hostler connects the 220-volt roundhouse power cable to the rusted engine, it begins to move. Before it can be stopped, the aged locomotive crashes into the turntable pit, fouling the turntable and trapping the Deer Lodge wrecker inside. All shop forces can do is start cutting up the motor where she lays. Torching apart the 10303 takes the better part of three days, while nothing can move in or out of the roundhouse. This motor, which would have been numbered E13, if it had not been wrecked, comes the closest of any electric to being a Jinx engine.

The extra unit spliced into the middle of the EF-2 and EF-3 classes in the 1930's, gives the King of the Rails 4500 continuous horsepower and the kind of pulling power that won't be found on most other railroads for many years, until the wide-spread use of diesel-electric power. Number 10506A,B&C is seen climbing the grade above Avery on Big Dick Creek bridge. The unit is rated for 2650 tons on this hill, sufficient power for handling 60 to 70 cars.

Milwaukee Road— R. Janin Collection

There are bright occasions in the 1930's such as the circumstance of this photograph, taken in 1937 at Avery; Alfred B. Butler, the photographer, was taking his wife on a honeymoon on the *Olympian.* Simple articulated steam engine No. 9311, which carried the train across the gap between electrified districts, backs toward the roundhouse. A big Westinghouse motor prepares to do battle with the cloud-covered Bitterroots, as a young Mr. and Mrs. Butler prepare to re-board the train for a memorable ride to Harlowton.

A. Bruce Butler Coll

bur C. Whittaker

Just how complicated the numbering of Milwaukee electric locomotives can get is illustrated by the E70 set, shown at Tacoma shortly after the general renumbering of 1939. These motors came into existence as the 10103A&B, of the EP-1 class. When that class was converted to freight service in 1920, they became Nos. 10233A&B of the EF-1 class. Now they are the E70A&B. In October 1942, they will become Nos. E48A&B before again becoming the E70A&B in November 1943. In August 1950, they will be renumbered E69A&B.

Next, in February 1953, they will become the E22A&B of the new EP-1A class. The histories of some motors are even more complicated, especially when two units take diverging paths in the renumberings.

(Below) Easier to keep track of are the four ES-2 switchers delivered in 1916 and 1919. These locomotives simply exchanged their 10050-53 numbers for the E80-83 designations. The 84-ton E82 is pictured here at Deer Lodge.

Two Photos— Ron V. Nixon

ISLAND OF SERENITY

The westbound *Olympian*, standing at the depot in Three Forks during April 1940, is showing definite signs of modern-inity in its orange and maroon consist. Montana is still the American stronghold for isolationism and non-involvement in foreign affairs, but soon even this quiet island of serenity will disappear. Across the Atlantic, the people of Britain fight for their lives against the German *Luftwaffe,* and the warlords in Japan are completing preparations for seizure of the Pacific. Passenger motor E15 carries its new number designation received in March 1939, along with a new venting system for the train boiler and "racing" stripes on its sides.

(Lower Left) The war clouds gathering in Asia and Europe are nowhere in sight on April 18, 1941, when Ron V. Nixon travels to St. Regis to record the last run of the Northern Pacific's Wallace Local. We note the low-slung Pacific, No. 2212, waiting for the passage of the eastbound *Olympian* behind motor E15. As soon as the premier train has slipped by, the Local will head out over the Milwaukee mainline to Haugan, where it will begin its own twisting climb over the Bitterroots. Disastrous floods in the 1930's washed out the NP line between St. Regis and Haugan, thereby bringing about a trackage rights agreement between the two roads.

(Below) The coming war that is to change everyone's life will soon end the delightful open air rides through Montana Canyon aboard the vista cars, making this more graceful way of life seem a terribly distant relic of the past.

Milwaukee Road

All— Ron V. Nixon

THE RACE

In 1941, Ron V. Nixon gets an opportunity that comes only once in a great while. . . the chance to photograph action on two favorite railroads simultaneously. Such is the occasion on April 14, as Nixon stands near the Bonita tunnels of both the Milwaukee Road and the Northern Pacific. Bearing down on him are the eastbound premier trains of both railroads; the 11-car *Olympian* and the 12-car *North Coast Limited*, racing across the Montana countryside, east of Missoula, in the last days of pre-war America. The Westinghouse motor is un-identified, but Nixon clearly sees that his favorite 4-8-4, No. 2611, is on the point of the *North Coast Limited*. As the trains rush past, we see their open platform observation cars, each with its own railroad's drumhead on the rear. Both trains had similar schedules at this time, and 'races' were not uncommon.

As to which train was winning the race, Nixon later says: 'At the time it seemed like a dead heat. But if I remember correctly, the NP was pulling up just a little.'

We moved to Whitehall in 1920. Piedmont was only three miles away, and my brother, Maynard, and I used to climb to the top of the NP coal dock and look through a cheap telescope to see which motors were standing at Piedmont.

One day when I was about 11 years old, I walked to Piedmont to attempt to make a drawing of No. 10235. Looking over my shoulder was engineer Walter Rowland, called to help a westerly train with that particular motor. He asked if I'd like to take a ride. I couldn't believe it, but didn't hesitate in the least. We got up in the cab and fireman Markel came and asked for my name and address, 'in case you get killed.'

I don't think there was ever a happier kid in the world than I was, riding the 10235 up to the Continental Divide. Markel asked if I wanted to pick up the orders at Donald. . . so I got down on the front platform and grabbed the orders from the lady operator. . . which I still have.

Over the years that I've been dealing with the Milwaukee, I've never known a better bunch of people. —Ron V. Nixon

If you didn't care about breaking rules, you could make a Westinghouse roll so fast it would beat anything on wheels. The controller had shunt positions, to weaken the traction motor fields and give you more speed, when speed was more important than power. Where a GE had one, a Westinghouse had two; and a third shunt you could only use when you went into regeneration. When you were running a Westinghouse wide open in the second shunt, you could put it into regeneration and it would come up into a third shunt. Now the motor was set to regenerate and slow down as you closed the throttle. Instead, though, you would leave the throttle wide open and keep motoring. Then you would get going faster instead of slower. You could get your train up to 90 miles per hour on level track like that. It was strictly against the company rules, though. It was hard on the traction motors and might create a flash-over. Bill Brautigam was the master mechanic and a pretty smart guy. You could flash-over a traction motor and he could tell just what you had been doing, even though he wasn't there. —W.H. Merrill, told to Noel T. Holley

World War II breaks like a tidal wave across the electrification, with a sudden tremendous flow of men and material westward to ports of embarkation along the Pacific Coast, the closest continental U.S. ports to the Orient. The December 7, 1941, disaster at Pearl Harbor, and the rapid advance of the Japanese armies in the Pacific, bring an urgency to electric operations unmatched in history.

(Above) Troop trains, like Extra 684 West, thunder through Easton, Washington, with more soldiers for the Pacific war, passing freights like Extra E71 West, also headed for the coastal ports.

(Lower Left) On July 9, 1944, a brand new General Motors 5400 horsepower freight diesel is tested on the Rocky Mountain Division. The No.42 rolls westward past Drexel, headed for the Idaho Division, where it will help speed freight traffic on the 210-mile gap between electrified districts. Like the electrics, these FT sets will help the U.S. to win the war in the Pacific. Although they do not pose an immediate threat to electric operations, they will be returned to GM in little more than a decade, and emerge as GP9 roadswitchers, which will be very direct challenges to its existence.

In the October 1972 issue of *Trains* magazine, retired Pullman conductor William M. Moedinger told a story about a memorable ride over the Rocky Mountain Division on Christmas Day 1945.

Shortly after dark, we pulled into Deer Lodge where the train was scheduled to be serviced. After the Christmas dinner in which I had just indulged, I needed exercise. The evening was clear and cold. I stepped down from the last sleeper and walked forward to the engine. With each step there was a crunch as my foot compacted the inch or so of snow on the ground. The steam engine had pulled away from the train, and electric power was backing down. I had never ridden a Milwaukee electric; perhaps this was my chance. I walked up to the lead unit, where the engineer was leaning out of the door. Before I had an opportunity to ask, he invited me up into the cab, which seemed full of smoke. Would I ride to Butte with them? He didn't have to twist my arm.

As soon as the highball came, the big electric began to ease the train out of the yard. Would I take over as soon as we cleared the yard limit? No the engineer was not kidding. Something was wrong with the oil burner which made steam to heat the cars, and unless he and his fireman got the burner functioning, those 16 cars in tow were bound to freeze up. I knew how to stop a train, didn't I? I knew the standard whistle signals, didn't I? When the hogger had the train rolling at about 35 mph, he got up and told me to take over. He showed me how to notch up the controller, and then he and the fireman disappeared to the rear. Ever so slowly, I notched up the handle until the indicator hand rested on 40, where I was to keep it. If only there were more grade crossings. Nobody would ever believe I had been the engineer of the **Olympian** *on Christmas Night, 1945. Ahead, a rabbit hopped across the track, so I gave it the customary two longs, a short, and another long. Well before Butte, the engineer and fireman returned. I relinquished my post. The engineer said I had done very well, and he thanked me. What's more, my whistle artistry had brought home to him how many grade crossings he had been missing over the years. During the pause at Butte, I walked back to my sleepers. My porter thought I had been left behind in Deer Lodge. I didn't explain; nobody would believe it anyway. Christmas 1945. I will never forget it.*

The Milwaukee and other railroads carry 90 percent of the nation's wartime freight, allowing the country to fight a two-ocean war. The one freight and one passenger train operations of the Depression have yielded to a flood of movements.

(Above) High in the Cascades, at Hansen's Creek trestle, Extra E25 East grinds up the grade with another freight train loaded with manufactured goods and forest products originated on the Pacific Coast. Many times during the war, tired boxcab engineers will coax their overloaded GE's over the mountain grades at just 7 or 8 miles per hour, running in Full Series in the 17th notch of their throttles.

(Below) A long *Olympian* rolls eastward near Bonner Junction, headed for Deer Lodge, behind the E12 motor. It is October 12, 1942, and Allied armed forces are in retreat all over the world. But within weeks the tide will begin to turn, after the coming battles at El Alamein and Stalingrad. The mysterious loads coming across the electrification, headed for the Hanford branch, will only be understood in 1945 when atomic bombs blossom out in the skies of Japan.

Warren R. Magee

78—BEVERLY-HANFORD.			
415	Ms	*October, 1938.*	416
■AM	....	(*Pacific time.*)	■PM
⬛11 35	0	lve..**Beverly** ⅄. arr.	6 1
11 40	1.0	**Beverly Junction.**	6 0
f11 55	4.8	..... Levering	f5 4
f12 25	15.6	... Priest Rapids ...	f5 1
f12 45	22.3	.......Vernita.......	f4 5
f1 00	25.3	..... Riverland.....	f4 4
f1 15	28.4	.... Haven	f4 3
f1 30	31.4	......Allard.......	f4 2
f2 00	38.4	+..White Bluffs..⅄	f4 0
2 30	46.2	arr..**Hanford** ⅄.lve.	⬛3 3
P M	....	ARRIVE] [LEAVE	P M

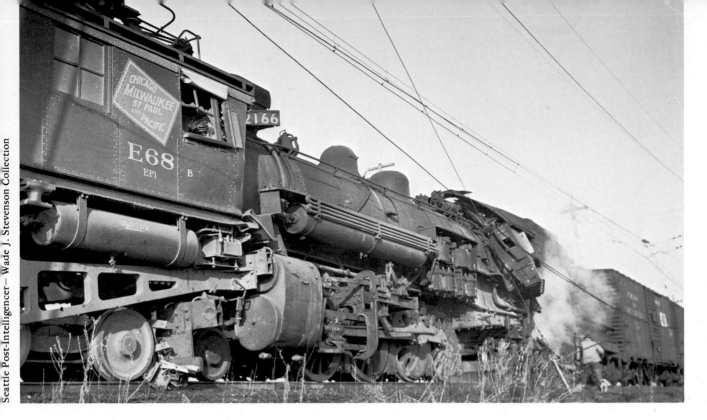

Seattle Post-Intelligencer— Wade J. Stevenson Collection

The Milwaukee's first passenger motors meet their end in the mid-1940's in this cornfield meet on joint track near Auburn, Washington. The UP 2-8-2 struck the E68 set, the former 10100 motors, which saw the first light of day at GE's Erie Works in 1915. They will be hauled back to Tacoma and cannibalized for parts until 1951, when they will be among the first of the old GE's to be scrapped.

(Below) Passengers on the eastbound *Olympian*, whipping along the Clark Fork near Tarkio behind the E17 and E12, must wonder what happened to Northern Pacific 4-6-6-4 No. 5140. Its the middle of June 1943, and the big engine derailed after hitting a broken rail at speed.

Ron V. Nixon

CHANGE IS IN THE AIR

(Right) As WWII ends, the King of the Rails is beginning to look a bit tired, as exemplified by this EF-3 set in Avery yard. Change seems to be in the air. Yet, as the engineer notches out his throttle, the old E36 faithfully responds, and soon the train is moving slowly up the canyon of the North Fork.

(Below) One of the veterans nearing the end of his career is Harold Theriault, on the E50 motor at East Portal. The boy who was laid off when the electrics came, has become their most staunch supporter. Harold's engine is the ex-10200 set, which made the first official run, on November 30, 1915.

(Bottom) The number E13, the former 10304, was retired after this wreck of the eastbound *Olympian* on March 17, 1947, at Soudan, just east of Alberton. The big mudslide was extremely damaging to the locomotive, but the injuries to the passengers were slight.

Wilbur C. Whittaker

Harold Theriault Collection

Bill McKonkey Collection

The youngsters of the early days are growing old, as we see with engineer James A. "Hooter" Drake, the master of the air brake on the Rocky Mountain Division. Standing to the left of Drake is his young fireman, Bill Lintz, who will go on to become a very notable figure in electrification history.

I never did know why they called him 'Hooter.' He came out West just before the railroad was completed, and was already in his sixties when I went firing. He was an artist with the air brake; he could come into the terminal at 30 miles an hour and stop right on the spot. Several times, because of regeneration failure, we came rolling down into Avery with only about 50 pounds of air left, and still stopped at just the right spot. I learned a lot about handling trains from him. He used to say, 'Keep your train stretched and you'll make good time, naturally.'

Once, while we were still in helper service, we stopped at DeBorgia to eat and had to climb through a right of way fence. I was about 30 years old and he was 66 years old. As I climbed through the fence, he said, 'Why is a young fellow like you doing that?' Then he put one hand on a fence post and jumped right over! I think he was in his mid-70's when he retired. The railroad had been his whole life. There were tears in his eyes as he asked about how things were going on the railroad, the last time I saw him in Missoula, before he died —Adam Gratz, engineer

NEW PHOTOGRAPHER ON THE COAST

It is fairly doubtful that anyone gives a second look to the skinny young kid alighting from the *Olympian.* Wade J. Stevenson is all alone that day in 1946 when he steps down from the train in Othello, to start a new career and life in this small Eastern Washington town.

Stevenson is from a railroading family in Indiana. The previous year he had taken off for the West, working a year for the Santa Fe at Winslow, Arizona. But the Milwaukee's electrification has lured him northward, and now he is going to start a new job as electrician at the Othello roundhouse. In 1946 this is still a busy meeting place for steam power, coming off the Gap, and for electric power coming in off the Coast Division.

It is not long before Wade begins his heavy photo-taking and record-keeping regimen. For the Coast Division, he is a new Asahel Curtis . . . "that guy from Othello who takes all those pictures." For fans of the electrification, he simply is the most avid photographer in Washington, with an interest that is to last even longer than the electrics.

(Right) The Erie-built Fairbanks-Morse passenger diesels came to the electrified districts in the summer of 1947, along with the new *Olympian Hiawatha.* Stevenson is on hand one morning at the Othello depot, to record the arrival of the westbound streamliner behind three units. Retouched photographs emanating from Milwaukee have already begun to depict a world where the F-M's are leading the 45-hour train across mountains devoid of decadent trolley wires. But instead, by mid-1949, the motive power shortage caused by a coal strike will bring about the laying-off of the photo retouchers, and keep the Fairbanks-Morse units east of Harlowton.

(Below) Working at Othello, Stevenson has opportunities to capture on film a number of unusual events. An example is the departure of today's westbound *Columbian.* With pantographs down, Bipolar E5 gets a tow out of town from F-6 Hudson No. 131, because of damage to the trolley system. The break in the trolley lies between Othello and the first substation, at Taunton, nine miles west, where the Hudson will be cut off.

(Below) The departure of today's 264 train from Othello, for the run across the Gap to Avery, is witnessed by a few roundhouse workers and the crew of the E64, which brought the train from Tacoma. The sharp-looking 1941 Plymouth sedan no doubt belongs to the operator on duty.

NON-PUBLICITY WEATHER

The tremendous publicity, that announced the electrification's final triumph over the snowy Cascade and Saddle Mountain barriers, occasionally proved to be in the category of overstatement.

(Right) On a very grim February 4, 1950, we note a greatly delayed westbound *Olympian Hiawatha* heading out into the storm, from Othello, behind No. E32 and Pacific 851. All five Bipolars are involved in the snow battle to the west, so it has fallen to the old EF-3 freighter to save the day. The tonnage reductions for steam in cold weather is something that doesn't affect engines powered by White Coal.

TONNAGE REDUCTION FOR WEATHER CONDITIONS.

Not Applicable to trains handled by electric power.

10 to 20 above........................ Reduce 10 per cent.	Zero to 10 below.................... Reduce 20 per cent.
Zero to 10 above.....................Reduce 15 per cent.	10 to 20 below.................... Reduce 30 per cent.

(Below) Then the 12-hour late *Columbian* grinds to a halt at the depot, behind the E70 freight motor. Mikado No. 726 has added little tractive effort to the battle over the grades to the west, but has provided steam heat for the no-doubt-frightened passengers.

All— Wade J. Stevenson

An out-of-control grass fire along the Milwaukee, near Othello, on June 24, 1949, seriously burns five men fighting the blaze. With great haste, a "mercy train" is assembled from an unidentified Bipolar and two cabooses. The nearest hospital is 74 miles away in Ellensburg, Washington. This quote, from the Ellensburg *Daily Record*, tells the story of the fastest dash ever made across the 2.2 percent Saddle Mountains grade. All of the men involved, with the exception of electrician Brown, survived.

A record-breaking trip was made by the Milwaukee Railroad special yesterday evening—93 minutes from Othello—to bring five victims of the grass fire there to an Ellensburg hospital.

The trip was made 23 minutes faster than the most hopeful prediction, and nearly 50 minutes faster than many railroad men thought it would be. George Johnston, master mechanic at Othello, had estimated the train would reach Ellensburg between 7:00 and 7:30 p.m. It reached here at 6:40 p.m.

A big electric passenger locomotive, the one that was to bring No. 17, the **Columbian***, west later in the night, was hooked to two cabooses. A train and engine crew, that had been called for a freight train, was switched to the caboose special and the run down Crab Creek to the Columbian was started.*

Railroad dispatchers at Tacoma cleared the line. Messages were sent ahead to Dr. J.P. Richardson, head of the Milwaukee medical services in this

section, to be prepared to take care of five badly burned men.

The accident happened near 4:00 o'clock in the afternoon. The special went over the west end switch in Othello yards at about 5:07 p.m. It literally flew across the Columbia River span at Beverly, then up the Saddle Mountain grade. Ninety-three minutes later, the 74 miles to Ellensburg had been covered.

Conductor Pete Hall and engineer Ed Dulock, both of Cle Elum—called the fastest engineer on the division—knew that the tracks were clear ahead. They knew that they would go around the diesel-operated eastbound streamliner **Olympian** *at Kittitas. They felt their one job was to get the suffering, badly burned men to Ellensburg, a hospital, and medical care.*

With its light load, the big electric passenger locomotive raced up the Saddle Mountains, through Rye, then through the tunnel at the summit, past Boylston and started down the valley. The streamlined **Olympian** *was waiting on the main line at Kittitas. The switches were set to route the hospital special via a sidetrack, but there was no stop. The two cabooses flashed by the windows of the waiting streamliner. Records were being made.*

No one expected the special before 7:00 p.m., but at 6:30 the special raced through Kittitas and eased off to a stop in front of the passenger station at Ellensburg at exactly 6:40, one hour and 33 minutes out of Othello station.

Before and after World War II, the Milwaukee is the proud operator of an extensive business built around the ski lodge owned by the railroad at Hyak, at the top of the Cascade grade. Special trains are operated most winter weekends to the Milwaukee Ski Bowl, where skiing, ski instruction, and competitive skiing events are conducted. Three Bipolars are enough to protect the schedules of the *Olympians*, leaving two motors free for use with the skiers. The trains typically leave Tacoma, and Seattle, early in the morning, for the 2 & 3/4 and 2 hour trips, respectively, to the Ski Bowl.

(Below) Bipolar E1 sits out a blizzard at the Ski Bowl while waiting for the last skiers to come down off the Olympian Hill, and other ski runs, at this popular facility. One of the promotional themes is, "Let The Engineer Do The Driving," not bad advice on a snowy day like today.

(Right) Other favorite scenes to be found during those winters of Milwaukee ski train operation include views of the imposing substation at the east end of the two-mile Snoqualmie tunnel, and of the steam rotary plows clearing the rails after storms.

Three Photos— Wade J. Stevenson

What we call the Middle Period draws to a close in the late 1940's, with America's railroads going diesel-electric and Milwaukee management feeling little sympathy for an electrical system that seems to have outlived its usefulness. The electrics seem to be lumbering along at 30 miles per hour toward certain abandonment.

But such is not to be, because of the man above, and political conflicts far removed from the Northwest. The man is Laurence Wylie, named in 1948 to the position he always wanted. . . electrical engineer in charge of the electrification. Wylie will often be spoken of as a genius, in his eight short years of leadership. He will carry the cause of the electrics to the highest levels of management, and create innovations and changes that will carry the system well into the Space Age.

(Left) The big steel bridge across the Clark Fork, at St. Regis, thunders to the weight of the E18 and E10 with the westbound *Columbian* in fall 1949. Before long, under Wylie's improvement program, EF-5 freight motors weighing over one million pounds will be crossing this same bridge, along with other new classes of freight and passenger power.

I had a funny thing happen once when I was firing for 'Hooter' Drake. We were coming down the grade around Drexel when we noticed smoke coming from the roof of the motor. I climbed up through the little hatchway and saw it was some oily soot from the steam boiler burning.

I was a young buck, so I just got a broom and went up on top to sweep the stuff off before it caused some damage. When Hooter saw me, he just laughed, the way he did.

There I was standing on top of the motor, carefully sweeping off the burning soot, not too far from the electrical gear, as our passenger train came down past the substation at Drexel. Well, the operator turned me in for safety violations.

Old Bill Brautigam was hopping mad when we got off at Deer Lodge. I just told him I was trying to keep the fire from causing some damage. He was sure mad, but he couldn't really do anything about it. —Adam Gratz, engineer

COMING OF THE JOES

By 1948, The King of the Rails is past 30 years of age and Milwaukee management is torn over the question of whether to upgrade the electrification, or to scrap it and join the rest of America's railroads in dieselization.

It is ultimately fate, and the efforts of Laurence Wylie, that tip the balance toward retaining the electrification.

(Right) Forces far removed from the canyons of the Bitterroots have brought GE demonstrator GE750 into Avery yard. The former WWII allies have fallen out, and an "Iron Curtain" has lowered across Europe. As the Cold War begins, President Harry S. Truman places an embargo on the sale of strategic goods to the Soviet Union. The embargo catches GE in the middle of an order for twenty 5-foot gauge, 3300-volt locomotives for the Trans-Siberian Railway, originally placed in 1946. The GE750 is the first of the completed units to be converted to standard gauge.

(Lower Right) The GE750 is tested on both electrified districts, such as at Renton, on the Coast Division, where it heads a test train.

Somewhere, the motor obtains a nickname. . . "Little Joe," for the iron-handed Josef Stalin, premier of the Union of Soviet Socialistic Republics. All the Milwaukee must do to acquire the 20 powerful new locomotives is come up with a "spare" million dollars. However, money is tight, and the opposing views of Wylie and his Chicago management cause the transaction to bog down.

Wade J. Stevenson

I was on the initial test run of the GE750. The biggest problem was that the Little Joe couldn't handle the tonnage the engineers from General Electric said it would. The GE people had based all of their calculations on horsepower and hadn't taken tractive effort into account. As you know, a 4-wheel drive Jeep will go many places that a 400-hp sedan won't go. This is because the Jeep can get traction. The Little Joe would slip its drivers with a train that the boxcabs could start, and the boxcabs could out-pull the Little Joe in the 15-18 mph speed range. All in all, the tests went poorly. Some of the people from the mechanical department pronounced the new locomotive less valuable than a GP-7. In the end, time proved them wrong.
—T. Barry Kirk, former Chief Electrical Engineer, as told to Noel T. Holley.

They're great engines. But when those Little Joes first came out here, everything in the darned cab was marked in Russian lettering. I don't think even the traveling engineers knew for sure just what was what. We'd just hope we knew what we were doing by the time we got out of the yard.
—Rocky Mountain Division engineer

Warren Wing Collection

Philip C. Johnson

No. E71, on a westbound train at Alberton, illustrates the early use of Little Joes on the Rocky Mountain Division. In this vintage period they are also used in the mountains as single-unit helpers. To get the most mileage from the Joes, management decides to restrict them to this electrified district, allowing the shorter and less busy Coast Division to stay in the keep of boxcabs and Bipolars.

After three of the would-be Russian motors are sold to the Chicago, South Shore & South Bend Railway, Wylie is finally able to get back to the bargaining table, but not before five units are sold to the 5-foot 3-inch gauge Paulista Railway of Brazil. The Milwaukee is able to obtain only twelve of the motors, in "as is" condition, for the $1 million originally asked for all 20 units.

(Left) The E75 and the eight other Joes built to broad gauge are converted to standard gauge in Milwaukee. Fresh out of the paint shops, No. E75 faces the Wisconsin sunlight with its trucks narrowed to fit American rails. Parts for another Joe to be re-gauged wait on an adjacent flatcar.

Two of the Joes, the E20 and E21, will become members of the new EP-4 class of passenger engines. The ten remaining motors will compose the numbers E70 to E79 of the EF-4 class. Demonstrator GE750 becomes the E70. The new Joes enter service in the West in the fall and winter of 1950, all as single-unit motors.

(Below) Shortly thereafter, the new orange and maroon Little Joe paint job is applied to other electric motors, and Bill Brautigam and the Deer Lodge shop forces create the first semi-permanently coupled Joe pairs. One of the first two-unit sets is seen on train No. 264, pausing at Alberton. An eastbound "dead freight" waits behind the E27 set.

The 11,060 horsepower one-hour rating of the EF-4 pairs exceeds that of seven contemporary F7 diesel units. In later years, the Joes will be ballasted to bring their weight up from 273 tons to 293 tons. The 311-ton EP-4's will be single-ended in the 1950's to make room in the rear cab for a steam boiler. Later, the installation of new J-R breakers will cause the single-ending of all Little Joes.

As an employee once said, "The money they paid for the Little Joes was the best money this railroad ever spent!"

Milwaukee Road

77

The 1949 Chicago Railroad Fair, and the return of the *Olympian Hiawatha* and *Columbian* trains to electric operation, are among the reasons for a new "winged" Bipolar paint job produced this year.

Not long afterwards, you step aboard the orange and maroon **Olympian Hi** *in Seattle to get a feeling for mainline electric passenger travel in the West. Leaving town, you head eastward, like the train above, under the section of trolley added in 1927.*

Milwaukee Road— R. Janin Collection

As in this publicity photo, passengers are already filling the Superdome cafe/lounge as the coastal cities slip away behind the beaver-tail observation car and the ascent of the steep canyons of the west slope of Snoqualmie Pass is begun in earnest.

It is late in May of 1950, about one month before a force of soldiers from a small Asian nation invades its neighbor to the south; a country named Korea. But such thoughts are still in your future, and your afternoon departure from Seattle has put you into Othello just after sunset. You step down from your Milwaukee-built sleeper and walk forward, in the twilight, to see Bipolar No. E4 being traded off in favor of the large steam engine that will haul your train tonight across the 225-mile Gap.

(Below) You fall asleep in your berth, happy and sound, long before your 4-8-4 has taken on a helper for the climb to Manito, and made the station stop at Spokane. All you recall are the occasional sounds of unsynchronized exhausts, and the distant whistling for dark country crossings in the forested hills of Eastern Washington and Idaho.

Avery is a sleepy blur of lights, voices, and dark mountains. The gentle clickity-clack of the wheels finally wakes you after sun-up, as your train rolls smoothly along the Clark Fork, approaching the station stop in Missoula.

(Right) At Butte, your train rolls down past the switch at Colorado Junction, and then backs into the stub-end passenger station. In the beautiful **Hiawatha** *observation car, the rear brakeman has his hand on the air valve as you crawl tail-first into the depot of this still tough mining town.*

(Below) You open your sleeping car's vestibule window as your eastbound **Hiawatha** *eases into Harlowton, where it meets its westbound counterpart. Number 15 is ready to depart behind motor No. E17, while F-M diesel No. 6 rests in the side pocket, after its dash from Chicago. Soon motor E15 will be taken off of your train and you'll begin your 1340-mile non-electrified ride to Chicago.*

You have left behind North America's longest railroad electrification. It's a trip you will always remember, an island of peace encountered before your life, and that of the electrification, is changed by the events which will transpire a month later on the other side of the world. —Author

Railway Negative Exchange

John C. Illman

The assignment of the Little Joes to Rocky Mountain Division passenger and freight runs in late 1950, coincides with the increased traffic brought about by the U.S. "police action" in Korea. However with only twelve Little Joes on 440 miles of railroad, they are sometimes quite scarce, as at Avery in September 1951.

This superb photograph by Philip C. Johnson of Missoula, depicts non-Joe action all through the yard. A four-unit freight diesel, in the distance, at left, prepares to head out over the Gap, while the two-unit E49 is preparing to act as a helper unit for an eastbound train. Hudson No. 132 is out-smoked by the steam boiler of Westinghouse motor E14 on the eastbound *Columbian*, one of the deficiencies of design of the EP-3 class. In addition to sporting a new paint job, No. E14 still proudly carries on its side the plaque commemorating the ride of President Warren G. Harding upon this locomotive on July 2, 1923.

hilip C. Johnson

One night my wife and I were asleep at Avery, and a sharp rap came at the screen window. 'Wilcox is dead!' That voice, saying that, has stuck in my memory all these years. That's all he said.

I got dressed and went down to the round-house. Wilcox, the night foreman, had been electrocuted on top of the Ell. A metal flashlight he'd been holding touched a lowered pantograph, while the other was still up.

What a night! — Roy E. Peterson, round-house foreman

The boost that the Little Joes give to the Rocky Mountain Division is hard to overstate. The GE boxcabs, now 35 years old, came to the Milwaukee when compound Mallets were the latest thing on American railroads. The day of the simple articulated steam locomotive was only dawning when the first Westinghouse motor came aboard in 1919. The Joes did not join this isolated island of antiquity until F7 and GP7 diesels were well on the way to dominating American railroading.

However, when the Little Joes did arrive, it was like the U.S. Cavalry racing in at the last moment in a Western movie. We see the effect at Harlowton in the early 1950's, where we find the westbound *Olympian Hiawatha* rolling into the station behind passenger F-units. Meanwhile, Joe E20 waits in the pocket, ready to take No. 15 out onto the 440 miles of mountain running to Avery.

These are great days on the Rocky Mountain Division . . . basically still an all-electric railroad.

In the dark recesses of the Harlowton round-house, a welder works at enlarging the front decks of the E29 set, the same old mountain battler that operated in the 1930's as the No. 10506. Behind the E29, one of the massive Westinghouse motors waits for its next call to duty.

With the occasional exception of the passenger Joes, the electric motors typically are dispatched in both directions from Deer Lodge, shuttling back and forth between there and the end terminals at Avery and Harlowton.

The Russians really missed something when the deal fell through for the Little Joes. With 5500 horsepower at 3300 volts, they would have been the Pennsylvania Railroad GG1's and E44's combined, for the Trans-Siberian Railroad. Can't you see a pair of these motors running at 50 or 60 miles per hour across a **Dr. Zhivago** *landscape in the dead of one of those Siberian winters? They would have been everything a comrade yardmaster could have asked for. —Author*

THE **MILWAUKEE** ROAD

The Little Joes give a big boost to freight operations on the Rocky Mountain Division, where standard power has been vintage boxcabs capable of attaining 15 miles an hour on the grades and 30 miles an hour on level ground.

(Left) Train No. 263, rolling into Harlowton from the east behind F7's in the early 1950's, encounters a still all-electric Rocky Mountain Division. Switching of the hotshot freight is accomplished by No. E56B, a 1916 graduate from GE's Erie locomotive works. These single-unit switchers are placed in the ES-3 class.

(Below) When train 263 gets rolling westward again toward Three Forks and Deer Lodge, it is in tow behind the E71 and E70 combination. The white flags show No. 263 is operating as an extra west today, an indication that the train is running ahead of schedule again.

THE BUTTE HELPER

The 21 miles of two percent westbound grade over the Continental Divide, at Pipestone Pass, is humbling to boxcabs and Joes alike. A pair of Little Joes is restricted to 2800 tons, and a three-unit boxcab set to 2250 tons. Because of this grade and the need for a helper on a westbound 4500-ton freight train, Jimmy Britzius has been called today to work the Butte Helper.

Before Britzius arrives on this beautiful spring morning in 1953, we note the eastbound *Olympian Hiawatha* rolling through Butte Yard, past the E37 and E52 motors assigned to the Butte Helper job.

Later, as Britzius takes charge of the E37 set, he takes the units to the east end of the yard for a meet with this morning's westbound *Columbian*, running behind the snow-splattered E10 motor.

Now the run over to Piedmont begins. As the west slope is ascended, our fireman looks out over the great Butte valley to observe the spidery black trestles of the Northern Pacific's Homestake Pass line in the far distance. A rush of cold air confronts the motors in the short tunnel near Grace, on the two percent descending grade.

At Piedmont, Britzius makes a perfect meet with Extra E36 West. Later the E37 will be cut into the middle of the Extra West and the six boxcab units will begin the slow grind back toward the summit of Pipestone Pass.

The Butte Helper: A Montana institution to last nearly as long as the trolley itself.

Electric helpers are commonly cut into trains so that the helper set pulls only slightly more tonnage than the road engine. The helper engineer can then tell almost exactly what notch the lead engineer's throttle is in, by watching his own ammeter and the meter indicating the voltage of the trolley. Knowing the amount of voltage drop, and comparing it to the grade and to the current he is pulling, the experienced helper engineer knows just what is happening 40, 50 or 60 cars ahead. —Author

FAINTLY FOREIGN

The inventive genius of Laurence Wylie, chief electrical engineer, is called upon again in 1952, as he attempts to find a low-cost way to get passenger Joes E20 and E21 into freight service, without retaining the expensive-to-maintain Westinghouse motors. Wylie's answer is to take the 35-year-old E69A&B to Tacoma shops and return them to the general EP-1 configuration they had in 1916.

(Above) The outcome is the E22 set, of a new EP-1A passenger class. The motor is equipped with F7 Hudson roller-bearing pony trucks, a faintly foreign streamlined front end, and 71:29 gearing. The set is shown bearing down on the depot at Ringling, Montana, with the westbound *Hiawatha*.

(Left) Rebuilding of the E22 leads to creation of the E23 set, built from the E28A&B and E36C units. We see its prow being cleaned at Deer Lodge.

Adam Gratz adds a personal reminiscence:

Those EP-1A's were hard riding at speed. I was wheeling right along one day near Cyr, with an equipment special, when Dan O'Bannan, my fireman, had to go back to the trailing unit to check on the steam boiler. He was gone quite a while, but then came back.

'You'll have to slow this thing down. Those doors between the units are bypassing each other and they'll cut me in half!', O'Bannan told me.

I told him, 'You'll just have to get down like a football player and then when the doors are just right, jump! Besides, how could they cut something as big as you in half?'

He laughed, but I slowed down.

*The transfer of mail, and an occasional passenger, into the daily truck connection of the White Sulphur Springs & Yellowstone Park Railway was a regular event at Ringling. The schedule was listed in **The Official Guide**, along with the name of the president of this Milwaukee subsidiary, John Ringling North, of the noted circus family.*

*On one notable occasion, however, the arrival of a half-dozen people on the **Hiawatha** for the WSS&YP "train" connection caught everyone involved by surprise. The embarrassed truck driver put several passengers in the cab, and the rest in the back of the truck, where they had to sit on shipments of mail order catalogs and boxes of baby chicks for the jolting 20 mile ride to White Sulphur Springs. —Author*

Stevenson

Early in 1951, another improvement is made to the King Of The Rails. The No. E25 set, at the roundhouse at Othello, is the first locomotive to be assembled into a new EF-5 class. This new four-unit configuration gives the E25 a total weight of more than one million pounds, with 250,000 pounds of tractive effort. These lash-ups, combined with better banding of armature elements, create locomotives of 6000 continuous horsepower, capable of speeds up to 45 miles per hour. Wade J. Stevenson's cartoon illustrates the steam/electric duality of Othello in the early 1950's.

(Below) The Seattle skyline is still enhanced by the rounded contours of Bipolars on the Milwaukee passenger trains at Union Station.

BOXCAB DAYS ON THE COAST

The coming of the Little Joes to the Rocky Mountain Division has little effect on the down-to-earth operations of the Coast Division electrified district, still basically a boxcab and Bipolar railroad. But soon steam will be gone from the Gap, and the men and women of the Othello roundhouse, photographed by Wade J. Stevenson (shown crouched down at far left), will have their ranks decimated by the diesel blight.

(Below) Old Bipolar and steam engine headlights, gathering dust at the Tacoma shops, are indications of the changes being made to the two electrified districts in the mid-1950's. Korean War traffic has ebbed, allowing discontinuance of the *Columbian*. Westinghouse quill motors will soon be gone from the railroad, and now the Coast's Bipolars are undergoing rebuilding.

Wade J. Stevenson

(Left) The arrival in Butte of the mighty No. E10, with the east-bound *Columbian,* is one of the latter-day scenes of these great locomotives in passenger service.

(Right) This gloomy twilight scene catches Nos. E18 and E16 in a sombre mood at Deer Lodge, during the engine change for the westbound *Olympian Hiawatha.* These are the Senior Citizen days for these great motors. Soon the engineer of the E18 will notch out his throttle, and the *Hi* will be on its way to Missoula and the Coast. By the middle of 1957, both motors will be gone. Despire weak frames, pesky quill drives and smoky boilers, the Quills often will be remembered as wonderful locomotives.

HIAWATHA MEMORIES

Much of the romance of the Milwaukee Road electrification rode with the *Olympian* and other passenger trains, on which generations of travelers relaxed while the wonder of White Coal propelled them safely and smokelessly across the Western mountains.

(Below) This romance of electric railroading still surrounds the *Olympian Hiawatha* in the latter days of passenger service, as in this photo of the stopped westbound train at Butte in the waning light of a freezing spring afternoon.

(Left) Later comes the station stop at Deer Lodge, the following summer. No matter that it grows dark; the dining car and the Milwaukee sleepers beckon us. For much of the night ahead, our almost-Russian Little Joe will pull us smoothly, quietly, and speedily toward Tacoma and the shores of the Puget Sound.

Along with the other improvements we were making to the electrification around 1955, I had the idea that we could improve the performance of the electric locomotives by raising the voltage output of the substations to as high as 3400 volts. This would reduce the voltage drop between substations, which approached 30 percent at times, and would potentially increase the horsepower of the locomotives 13 percent.

I requested permission from management to make the change. It was refused. The 'experts' said that the electrical problems resulting from the voltage increase would offset anything that was gained. But I was sure it would work, and went to the substations on the Coast Division and instructed

the operators how to shim the back of the main field poles of the m-g sets. This increased the field flux and increased the output voltage by several hundred volts. At the same time, we adjusted the voltage meters to read 3000 volts at the higher output.

This worked very well, without any problems. It improved the performance of the boxcabs quite a bit. So I went back to management and finally got permission to make the change. We did the same thing to the substations on the Rocky Mountain Division and then went back to the Coast Division to adjust the meters to read right.

—Laurence Wylie, as told to Noel T. Holley

Wade J. Stevenson

BIPOLAR IMAGE

In a classic portrait of Eastern Washington rail-roading, doubleheaded Bipolars head west out of Othello with a very late *Olympian Hiawatha* on Christmas Eve 1955. The storms sweeping in from the Gulf of Alaska have been heavy, and the E4 and E2 have their work cut out for them on the snowy rails of the Saddle Mountain crossing despite beneficial cooling effects of cold weather on the pair's two dozen traction motors. Near the depot, the GP9's that brought No. 15 across the Gap prepare to head for the roundhouse. This is the swan song for the Bipolars on the Coast. Now completely rebuilt, they will be brought to the Rocky Mountain Division to handle the remaining passenger traffic on that district. For the second time in its history, declining patronage has caused the demise of the *Columbian.*

(Below) Another development of the mid-1950's is the electrification of the Milwaukee snow fighting service, brought about through elimination of steam power in rotary plows. Instead, the blade wheel of rotary X900212, moving out of Avery ahead of the E34 and a GP9 rotary power unit, is driven by a salvaged pair of GE boxcab traction motors. This gives Milwaukee Road's rotary plows greatly improved performance and eliminates dependence on water and oil supplies.

Milwaukee Road

THE INGENIOUS MISTER WYLIE

In 1958, two years after his retirement from the Milwaukee, Laurence Wylie makes one of the most important contributions to the perpetuation of the electrification; the little cab-mounted controller that allows electric locomotives to multiple-unit with diesel-electric "boosters." It is Wylie's answer to the hordes of new GP9 roadswitchers threatening the electrification, the newest representatives of the technology that caused the abandonment of most other North American electrification projects. These devices allow the throttles of the diesels to be set proportionately to those of the electrics. A removable link allows the engineer to control either type of power independently.

(Above) The new development allows such scenes in the Bitterroots as westbound freight No. 263 dropping down from St. Paul Pass, across Kelly Creek trestle, with double Joes and a GP9

booster. The additional tractive effort of the Geep allowed the Joes to handle 3600 tons over the Rocky Mountain Division without the need of a helper. The same technique now allows eastbound trains of up to 5800 tons without helper.

(Lower Right) The Wylie controller works equally well with more than one GP9 booster, as we see at Avery, where a heavy No. 263 train drops down into the yard.

Other Wylie-directed improvements include automation of most of the 22 substations on the two electrified districts. This allows an operator at one station to remotely control the operations of other substations on the line. At East Portal, in the Bitterroots, we note the remote control panel by which this substation controls operations at Primrose, Tarkio and Drexel substations.

Ted Benson

CEDAR FALLS PASTORAL

The little helper station of Cedar Falls, Washington, at the foot of the Cascades climb, is one of the delightful anachronisms of the Milwaukee electrification around 1960. Here, only 40 miles east of Seattle, we find time at a stand-still. Deer graze behind the old milk-loading dock of the company bunkhouse, knowing, perhaps, that their only threat will come with the arrival of the evening branch-line train from Everett. The bunkhouse lobby is a relic from the 1920's, marred only by the presence of a television set.

Warren Marcus and I were amazed to find the old Cedar Falls bunkhouse and restaurant still operating in the manner of the first World War. It was as if the electrification had just been built. After we had finished eating, I told the cook I'd like to pay for the meal and lodging together.

I asked, 'How much?'
He said, 'That will be $2.25.'
I asked, 'How much for the hotel?'
He said, '75 cents a night.'—Author

(Left) Near the front door is a knife switch, by which tired snowplow operators or helper crewmen can summon the clerk.

(Above) One of the evening's chores for the 81-year-old cook is to feed the family of raccoons that reside permanently beneath the kitchen steps.

(Below) As midnight approaches, the weather is fit only for the building of arks, as heavy rains fall on the E25 set while it switches a helper into train No. 264. The downpour is accompanied by snow at upper elevations, and by gale-like winds, which moments later, again topple the author's camera into the mud.

	Ruling grade	EP-1 EP-2	EP-3	EP-4 EF-4	EF-1	EF-2 EF-3
Avery-East Portal	1.7	1250	1150	1600	1750	2650
East Portal-St. Regis	Down					
St. Regis-Deer Lodge	0.4		3500	5400	6000	9000
Deer Lodge-Alloy	0.6		3000	4050	4500	6750
Alloy-Donald	1.66	1400	1150	1600	1750	2650
Donald-Lombard	Down					
Lombard-Cardinal	0.46		3500	5400	6000	9000
Cardinal-Loweth	1	1600	1600	2400	2650	3975
Loweth-Harlowton	Down					
Harlowton-Valencia	0.6		3000	4050	4500	6750
Valencia—2 Miles West of Bruno	1		1600	2520	2800	4200
2 Miles West of Bruno-Loweth	2	1300	960	1400	1500	2250
Loweth-Lombard	Down					
Lombard-Piedmont	0.3		4000	7200	8000	12000
Piedmont-Donald	2	1050	960	1400	1500	2250
Donald-St. Regis	Down					
St. Regis-Haugan	0.8		1600	2520	2800	4500
Haugan-Roland	1.7	1250	1150	1600	1750	2650
Roland-Avery	Down					

EP-3 engines limited to 50 cars.

The beauty of Bipolar electric passenger service is as great on the Rocky Mountain Division in 1958 as it was on the Coast Division the three previous decades. The morning arrival of the eastbound *Olympian Hiawatha* at Missoula is recorded on a June day by Ron V. Nixon. Streamliner yellow E3 is on the point. An employees' timetable of the period gives tonnage ratings for these rebuilt Bipolars, as well as for the other classes of freight and passenger power.

(Below) On July 15, 1958, Philip C. Johnson, a Forest Service entomologist from Missoula, stands above the ledge at Soudan where the *Olympian* was derailed by a mudslide in 1947, to photograph the eastbound *Hi* coming out of the morning fog along the Clark Fork. Tacoma rebuild No. E5, with two windows in its center shroud, leads No. E4.

Two Photos— Ron V. Nixon

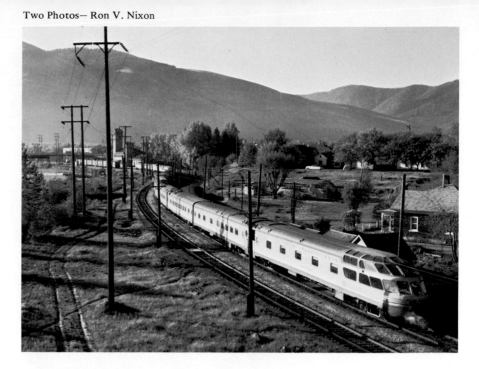

(Above) The last *Olympian Hiawatha* trains to operate west of Deer Lodge, pass through Missoula on May 23, 1961. The beautiful Skytop Lounge brings up the rear of final No. 15. On the point of the last No. 16, we see the diesels which replaced the Bipolars in 1959. The wonderful days of mainline electric passenger trains in the West are over. Of the great Bipolars deadlined at Deer Lodge, only the E2 will survive.

(Below) Nos. E5 and E4, which rolled out of the morning fogs at Soudan, are now deep in regeneration at Vendome, east of Butte, where Bill Merrill's train ran away on that dangerous fall night in 1920.

Philip C. Johnson

The 50-year-old E42 motors, dropping down a 1.7 percent grade in a Cascade rain forest, suggest aspects of electric railroading unique to North America.

Just as unique are the men who operate these trains. Take conductor Darrel DeWald, left, and engineer Jimmy Petersen. They're mountain men from Alberton, Montana. They are family men, reserved, confident, practical, and self-governing; men who know where they live, and why.

Darrel, whose grandfather came West with the railroad, is a union griever, respected by men and management. Jimmy, also from a Milwaukee family, is as smooth an engineer as ever notched out on a mountain grade. It was as if, in 1909, the Milwaukee had tried to create a new breed of railroader, by locating division points away from the major cities.

(Below) The small town nature of Alberton is shown by the turnout of almost the whole town for a high school girls' basketball game. Jumping is Jean Petersen, No. 22, the daughter, niece and granddaughter of Milwaukee employees.

AVERY HELPER: 1963

The Avery helper is a 40-year-plus institution on this spring afternoon in 1963. The crew board in the Avery roundhouse announces that Gratz and O'Bannan will take the E34 set to Haugan to help eastbound Extra E42A over St. Paul Pass.

Adam Gratz, the engineer, tosses his bag onto the trailing unit at the roundhouse. Gratz is the personable, fast-running engineer; the Mayor of Alberton, and defender of Little Joes.

In the cab of the E34B, Gratz reads his orders and notches out the throttle of the boxcab motors, passing the GP9's that brought the Extra into town from the Gap. Spare Joes E72 and E76 sit awaiting their next assignment. In typical Milwaukee style, the helper engine is cut into the middle of the train, so that each EF-5 set will be pulling and regenerating about the same amount of tonnage.

Starting up the canyon of the North Fork, clouds of sand begin to roll up from around the drive wheels of the E34. Not a filter is in sight as the sand sifts into all parts of the interior of the units.

Further up the hill we see the head end, and get a frightening look almost straight down into Loop Creek.

Deep inside St. Paul Pass tunnel the tension mounts, as Gratz decides whether to go into regeneration "the old way" or "the Brautigam way." There's a lunge as he decides on "the old way" and the traction motors begin to hold the train in check.

At Haugan, Gratz throws the siding switch so that fireman O'Bannan can run the E34 back up the hill. There's a brief stop at East Portal to deliver supplies to this snowbound little community. Then come the miles of "yang-yang" sounds as the E34 regenerates back down the long grade toward Avery.

After a few minutes less than seven hours on duty, Gratz and O'Bannan drop off the helper engine at the roundhouse and prepare for some rest. In 1963, this is just another day of normal operations for the Avery helper.

Seen from the top of the Avery roundhouse, the E34 waits for another call to duty in the spring of 1963.

We had a lot of real characters working the west end in those days, like the signal maintainer 'Redboard' Murray.

One day we were dropping down the grade into Avery and hit an unexpected red signal. But as we stopped, I noticed that the plug of a slide detector fence just ahead was pulled out. No rocks had fallen, just the plug was out.

The engineer, Pete Fous, thinking about Redboard's love of fishing, told me to just plug it back in and not to say a word.

As we pulled into Avery, the signal maintainer was out on the platform asking about our trip.

'Any problems?,' Redboard asked.

'Nope,' said my engineer.

'No signal problems?'

'Nope, green all the way.'

'Sure it was okay on the hill?'

'Yep!'

We really laughed later, seeing what we suspected were plans for a little paid fishing trip going down the drain.

—Adam Gratz, recalling his firing days

Radio to Gratz:

Conductor: 'Adam, aren't you going around these curves a little fast?'

Gratz: 'You must have your foot on the floorboards back there, because the headend went around them just fine!'

Ed Lynch Collection

There is an uneasy tension growing in the Tacoma round-house in 1963, as boxcab sets like No. E50 begin sharing stalls with the new second-generation GP30 diesels. Engine No. 342 packs 2250 horsepower of self-generated electricity into a carbody no larger than one of the electric units. Four-unit lash-ups of GP30's are running straight through from the Twin Cities on the newly-inaugurated high-speed freight trains, No. 261, the *XL Special,* and No. 262, the *Thunderhawk.* The lines of derelict boxcabs are growing, ready for the first wholesale scrapping in 1964.

(Right) The new balance that is struck between electric and diesel power is illustrated by eastbound train No. 262 leaving Avery. Little Joe E72, in a new "diesel" paint job, leads 13,000 roaring horsepower up the North Fork. The new pattern will frequently see electrics augmenting the diesels, rather than diesels helping electrics. All-electric trains will continue to operate, but the diesels are out West to stay.

(Left) A wreck in Montana Canyon in the spring of 1966 almost destroys the E78, requiring that it be sent east to Milwaukee Shops for rebuilding. When it emerges, the Little Joe will have F7 diesel-type cabs and a new air intake grille to set it apart from its fellow EF-4's.

BACK TO FREIGHT

The early 1960's on the Coast Division witness the end of passenger service and the conversion back to freight of the unique E22 and E23 passenger motors of the EP-1A class.

It has been quite a half-century for the E22 set. The units began life in 1916 as the 10103 passenger set, and were converted to freight motors in 1920. They became passenger motors again in 1953 and now, in 1961, are back to freight.

(Left) We find the newly converted E22 freight motors wheeling east out of Beverly, Washington, in 1964, heading for the end of trolley at Othello. This area between the Columbia River and the town of Othello is the only real "desert" crossed by the electrification. The E22 set will operate until 1968, and will be scrapped in 1973. It will be a strange, Cinderella-like life for these "faintly foreign" home-built motors.

(Below) Nightfall at Othello sees the four units of the E39 set ready to take train No. 263 off to Tideflats yard in Tacoma. The E39D unit retains its unusual styling, a holdover from the days when it was the E23C passenger unit.

COWBOY COUNTRY

Three Forks, Montana, is one of those quaint Western towns where electric trains fit right into the landscape. Across from the depot stands the Sacajawea Hotel, named by the Milwaukee in the 1920's for the Indian maiden who led the Lewis and Clark expedition to this point in the summer of 1805. A few miles further west, along the Lewis and Clark trail, cowboys of the Sappington Hereford Ranch still round their cattle up on horses at Willow Creek, while a pair of Joes stop to switch livestock cars.

Down at the depot, No. E29 pauses in its switching duties near the archway through which *Olympian* and *Columbian* passengers were led to the wonders of Yellowstone National Park. One of the Little Joes shows the signs of other than Montana origins, with welded-over buffer pockets still decorating its pilot beam.

Very late in the life of the Milwaukee electrification, two new photographers come out of the West to document the latter-days of the electrics.

One is a railroader, the other a newspaperman; one a careful worker in the Bob Hale tradition, and the other a fast-shooting journalist. However, both are very much alike in that they use 35mm cameras to create memorable and original images of the electric operations.

The first photographer is Max Tschumi, who works as a Canadian National conductor in Vancouver, British Columbia. Tschumi's trip to the Coast Division in October 1968, takes him out to Beverly, Washington, where he carefully photographs electric operations on Beverly Hill.

(Right) We note the E39A,D,C,&B set silhouetted against the mountains, while it waits on the east bank of the Columbia River for a helper to be added to its consist. Ahead is the 2.2 percent Beverly Hill, steepest mainline grade on the electrification.

(Below) Three weeks later, in October 1968, we see an extremely heavy sugar beet train headed west up the same Saddle Mountain grade. Even though the Columbia River bridge and Beverly Junction are just to the rear of the caboose, the old motors have already slowed to a walk on the heavy grade, probably running in Full Series. On the point is the four-unit helper, E42A&C and E49C&B. The road engine is the E50A, E35C and No. 50B. The sounds of traction motor blowers and gears fill the air as the units slowly pass the camera, hauling a load their designers could not have imagined.

Before dawn, on a cold November morning in 1968, Tschumi hikes into the rain forest of the Cascades, above Mine Creek trestle, to photograph a light engine, and a westbound freight train. He waits for more than four freezing hours on a tiny, precarious ledge above the bridge. Finally, at about 10 a.m. the two trains come...together. It turns out that the E50 helper engine had shorted out while returning to Cedar Falls, and was picked up by the E25 set and added to the consist of the freight. From front to rear the units are the E25A,D,C,&B, E50A, E35C, and E50B.

All— Max Tschumi

115

Tschumi battles his way into the isolated town of Avery, Idaho, in the winters of 1968 and 1970, to capture these unusual winter action pictures. Avery is still deep in the grip of winter, in 1968, as train No. 261 rolls in off the hill behind E75 and four new diesels. Little Joe E21, in the foreground, switches cars for a forthcoming train. In order to obtain the photos at right, Tschumi rode with the crew of electric rotary plow No. X900212, aboard the two GP9's that provided the propulsion for the train and electricity for the plow's operation. We first observe the flying snow as the siding at Falcon is cleared, then view the appearance at the east switch of train No. 261 behind Joe E73 and a trio of second generation diesels...beautiful photographs of electric power hard at work on February 18, 1970.

All— Max Tschumi

(Below) As the rotary plow passes the east switch at Adair siding, Tschumi looks down across Loop Creek Canyon to see the E72 leading train No. 263 across Turkey Creek trestle.

The month of March 1970 came in like a lion, depositing snow over most of the Rocky Mountain Division.

(Above) Steeple-cab switcher E80 shoves cars of limestone to the Anaconda plant at Butte, while the old Milwaukee depot and the mining skyline appear gaunt in the snow.

(Below) Joes E79 and E20 roll past the Butte yard office on an almost zero visibility morning, on the first of March. These photographs were grabbed at the last moment, as the westbound extra loomed up unexpectedly.

A tricky winter hike into the snowy hills, in the middle of the great loop above Vendome, yielded this photo of a heavy train descending the Pipestone grade behind a Joe and three diesel units. In the distance is the great valley of the Jefferson River, and the Tobacco Root Mountains.

The other new photographer is Ted Benson of Modesto, California, who makes his first photo-journalistic journey to the electrics in July 1972, by which time the proud E42A motor of Tschumi's Beverly Hill photographs is in ruins outside the Tacoma roundhouse.

(Above) Other unique images captured by Benson include Little Joe E74 on train No. 261, racing westward near Gold Creek on a warm July morning; running, as Benson says, "in grand defiance of BN and in grudging partnership with GM."

(Above Right) The remoteness of Milwaukee substation locations is exemplified by the station at Loweth, Montana, at the top of the Belt Mountains grade, where today's No.264 pays a visit behind Joes E79 and E70, and a trio of diesels. The 3400-volt trolley system will soon begin to accept regeneration from the 11,000 horsepower Joes, but the diesels will keep the output of their dynamic braking to themselves. The cut seen here is part of a 1957 line relocation that eliminated the short two percent grade up from Bruno that had been a problem for the boxcabs.

(Below Right) Inside the lunch room, on television, George McGovern is winning the 1972 Democratic nomination for President. Outside, in Avery yard, the E45 set prepares to head east behind the three GP40's of train 264. Problems with the Locotrol circuitry have made No. 264's diesel helpers inoperative. Therefore, the call went out for a locomotive that had only to raise its pantograph to start to work.

THE DURABLE E50

Time has touched the E50 set only lightly in the early 1970's. The E50A&B are the original 10200A&B motors that started out from Three Forks on the historic morning of November 30, 1915, with the first official train. Here we view E50 rolling into Avery, with train No. 263 under the direction of engineer Adam Gratz. Then the motor's headlight shines through the yard as Gratz spots his train for the diesels that will take it out over the Gap. Later yet, the E50A, E47C and E50B stand waiting for their next assignment at the Avery roundhouse. The E50A&B are not the oldest U.S. electric locomotives in terms of years, but have any other mainline electric locomotives in the United States ever grown so old in head-to-head competition with diesels? The electrifications of the Great Northern, the Norfolk and Western, the Virginian, and even the Butte, Anaconda & Pacific are now just distant memories. Yet, the Milwaukee's E50 rolls onward.

AVERY IS TOUGH

Avery is a quiet, beautiful mountain town that can drive you rip-roaring crazy in about four hours, unless you go out of your way to meet people and get into the intimate spirit of the place.

A tough trip in April, 1972, illustrates the problem.

Warren Marcus, Chuck Fox, and your author, drove 1000 miles to get there, with the last 26 miles of rock and mud-covered road almost pounding the car to pieces.

The bad news hits us in the 24-hour lunch room at the depot...the Idaho Hotel has collapsed from the snowfall...back country roads are closed by slides and heavy snow...and a slide at Stetson has closed the mainline.

In the morning, Chuck and I found out the railroad would be back in operation by noon. We'd come to take photos up by Loop Creek, so what else to do, but to start walking through the mud and snow?

By the time we'd gone twelve miles we were tired. It looked like one hell of a night coming up. No sleeping bags, or much of anything else.

But as we walked around that last curve into

Falcon...there in the hole was the E73 on train No. 265! Hooray!!!

The engineer was George "Blondie" Rainville. Hooray, again! It was two very tired cameramen that he carried back to Avery.

Our muscles were still sore and stiff later that evening as we watched a Joe set switching in the yard. The mountain had beat us. So had Avery. There didn't seem to be any way to get up into that snowbound country above Loop Creek in one piece.

But then an idea started to take form...

The engineer looked at my waiver and said "Okay." I rushed to toss a sleeping bag, cameras and food aboard the E21 just before it began moving out into the snowy mountains. Engineer Adam Gratz said that there was a section crew warming shack at the upper end of Falcon, that just might be unlocked. So I crossed my fingers.

Al Manuel, the brakeman, must have thought, "This guy is completely nuts," as I jumped off the moving E21 into the snow at Falcon. He tossed off my sleeping bag and food, and with a wave, was gone into the foggy night.

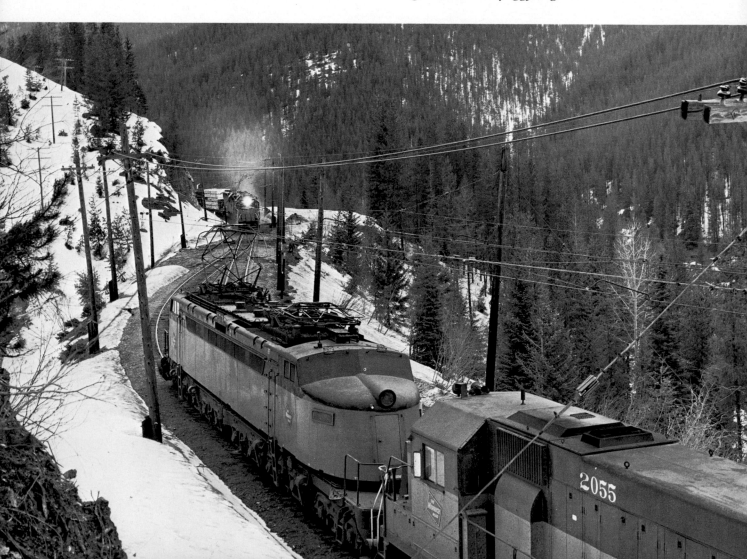

(Left) Train No. 265, with engineer Blondie Rainville, waits at Falcon, 12 miles above Avery, for meets with 1-261 and 2-261 as the railroad starts moving again, after the clearing of the slide at Stetson. It is April 1972, and this great Bitterroots wilderness area is still snowbound, the snows crossed only by the tracks of wild animals and the electrified Milwaukee mainline.

(Above) Double Joes, led by E21, get ready to pull out of Avery for the snowy mountains, and to carry the re-equipped author nearer to the trestles along Loop Creek.

(Right) In typical Avery hospitality, nobody gets turned away from the depot in winter, including the dog which has taken up residence beneath the trainmen's desk.

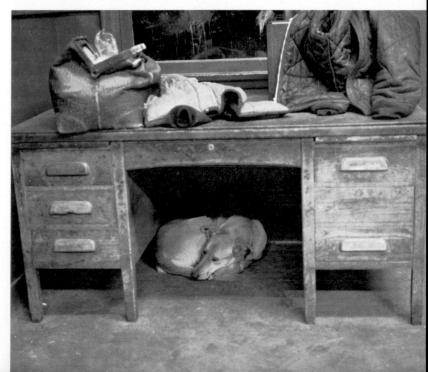

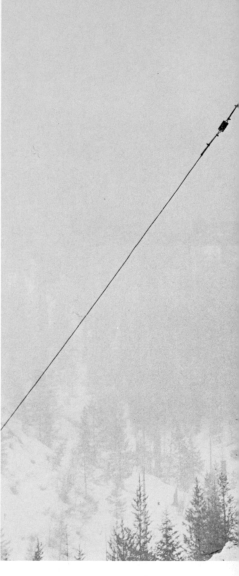

I checked out the shack in the snow and found that it was unlocked. That caused me to yell the third 'Hooray!' of the day.

After sleeping like a log, another shock came in the morning. It was snowing again! White tennis shoes looked pretty ridiculous about that time, but I headed out for the long hike to the high trestles beyond Clear Creek.

It was still snowing at No Name trestle, looking nothing like that beautiful scene photographed by Asahel Curtis in October 1929. Walking on to Turkey Creek trestle, about 3 miles, nothing was visible for several very cold hours. Then the sounds of the first train could be heard over the wind.

Finally train No. 265 appears, rolling off the bridge. It is in the charge of an old friend, the E45!

Snow is tracing a line around its front end, and more snowflakes dance around her, as she passes. Then the helpers come along; GE diesels 50 years junior to the E45! This isn't the picture-taking envisioned in California, but for the first time, it is worth all the effort.

(Left) Before I can get back to No Name trestle again, train No. 266 is upon me, Double Joes on the point!

It is hard to hold the camera steady, with the snow and wind. Like an idiot I take an extra shot and have to reload in the flying snow before the helpers come. There's only time for a following shot, but who cares?

It's not pleasant to recall the number of miles walked after those pictures. Getting a ride on a track car from the lower end of Falcon most of the way to Stetson helped a lot.

The last three miles of walking were through mud. I was so exhausted I stumbled once and fell on my face. Upon returning to Avery, I was very tired but happy. It was a tough trip. Thank you, Milwaukee Road! —Author

Chuck Fox

It was one of those cold and rainy days at Avery, but we decided to hop eastbound train No. 266 and ride to Alberton, just for the fun of it.

We were trying to act casual, but even old Harold Theriault was out on his porch waving a newspaper at us as we left town. Word travels fast in a place like that.

It got colder and colder as we headed up toward the pass. It started snowing and we were freezing ourselves silly.

When they cut out the boxcab helper at Haugan we couldn't stand it any longer in the boxcar, so we got onto a piggyback car. Man, that was worse yet! That steel beam I sat on never warmed up one bit in all of the hours I sat on it.

By the time we got to Alberton we were almost chilled to death. We were going to stay over, but when we saw No. 263 getting ready to head back to Avery we panicked, and got into the rear cab of the E50 to get warm.

There wasn't even time to get anything to eat, and we'd been out about 8 hours. But the worst part was that the damned 'foot warmer' electric heaters were on FULL in the cab.

We started frying.

We opened every window and door, but the heat was still intense. We didn't know how to shut it off, and nearly died of heat prostration before we got back to Avery.

It was two frozen/fried customers that fell off the train that night. We were destroyed...freezing eight hours one way...and baking eight hours the other way. We couldn't even eat by that time. Never ever again! —Railfan

The longest night comes for the Coast electrified district on November 14, 1972, with final moves of the E39 set.

Shown here are the motors shortly before the end, pausing in Cle Elum yard after a day's work inside Snoqualmie Pass tunnel. That same night, up at the summit at Hyak, we observe the work train used by the E39A,D,C and E47A units, along with the darkened portal of the summit tunnel in which they will work again tomorrow. Motor E39 was not chosen for this job because of its tractive effort, or beauty, but was picked because its non-poluting qualities suit the working conditions in the confines of the two-mile tunnel.

In the end it is the Gap, and the new radio-controlled diesel helpers, that bring the wire down. The increasing traffic from the opening of the new Portland, Sumas, Louisville and other freight gateways, because of the Burlington Northern merger, has only delayed the ending of electrification on the Coast.

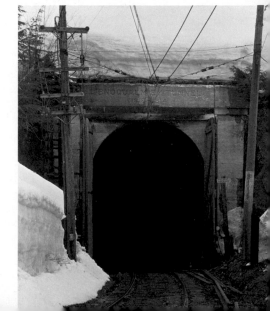

YOUNG BRYAN

Bryan Gustafson, a young man from a Milwaukee railroading family, and engineer of today's Avery helper, represents the new generation of trainmen who prefer an SD40-2 diesel to a boxcab any day. Yet, as we will see, Bryan is ultimately to earn a special place in the history of the electrification.

Today, however, is just another day for Bryan and his conductor, Lloyd Smith, as they wait for hours at Haugan for a No. 263 train that never seems to arrive. Because of problems at Alberton, it is almost sundown before Smith can lean out from the porch of the E29A and see the E75 and E78 coming into view.

The catenary glows from the light of the E29 set as crewmen prepare to cut in the helper. It is nearly dark by the time all the moves are made, and No. 263 can head off to Bryson for a meet with No. 1-262.

In the early 1960's a couple of carloads of grain went over the bank at Falcon. They laid there all winter under the snow. By the time spring came, the wheat was thoroughly fermented.

Not long after the thaw, a trackman was on the block phone to Avery from the phone booth at Falcon. He was talking away, and then suddenly started yelling, "Yi! Yi! Yi!" Then the phone went dead.

All of us were wondering what had happened. A few minutes later he came back on the wire.

It seems that while he was talking to us, he'd heard a noise behind him. He turned around to see a slightly woozy black bear standing over him on his hind legs, with his paws outstretched. The trackman was nearly scared to death.

What had happened was that the bears had been into that fermented mash, and had gotten just plain drunk.

The forest service let the Milwaukee sectionmen carry guns for a while, but the "bear revolt" was put down without a shot. The mash ran out and the sectionmen could work without constantly looking over their shoulders.

—Jim Lowery, as told to the author

THE MILWAUKEE ROAD

133

OCTOBER 31 DEADLINE

As fall comes to the high country of Montana in 1973, the word goes out: October 31 should see the end of mainline electric operations. The last boxcab helpers were taken off in mid-August, and the trolley has been dead west of Deer Lodge since shortly afterward. The "farwell" press trip has already been made behind Nos. E21-E20, from Deer Lodge to Missoula. It appears that only a miracle can save the electrics.

(Left) There seem to be only a few active days of service left for No. E20 and E21 as they head west through Jefferson Canyon, west of Three Forks, with train No. 263 and dead-in-tow No. E29. The boxcab is being returned to Deer Lodge after work train service. The trolley and feeder wires glisten in the afternoon sun, on the same route followed by Lewis and Clark 168 years earlier.

(Below) Just above Vendome the two percent grade of Pipestone Pass is engaged in full, and sand starts flying on the lower end of the horseshoe curve.

(Above, Right) A minute later, we witness, in silhouette, the Joes pulling hard as they pass around the top of the horseshoe curve.

(Below, Right) One half-hour later, at Donald, the landscape has already turned to winter.

The shiny, new General Motors SD40-2 Locotrol unit leading train 262 out of Butte yard acts like a new landlord coming to inspect his property, while 58 year old E81 resembles an older tenant keeping out of his way. It is the morning of October 31, 1973...doomsday for the electrification. It does not appear the the Arab oil crisis will prolong the life of the electrics. The arrival of these new diesels, and the lengthy period of final decision making, seems to guarantee that there will be no governor's pardon today.

(Right) Later that afternoon, at Missoula, a storm swirls around the famous old depot, while the dispatcher's phone line hums with talk about mainline diesel power.

(Far Right) At Deer Lodge, motor E82 seems to be winding up its operations during the storm, with two young groundmen ready for anything that comes.

Looking east from the yard at Deer Lodge, there is only the twin catenary and the steel rails converging upon a white horizon, beyond which only internal combustion power has any future, energy crisis or not.

Out behind the Deer Lodge roundhouse, Little Joes E72 and E75 already sit in storage under a gathering blanket of snow.

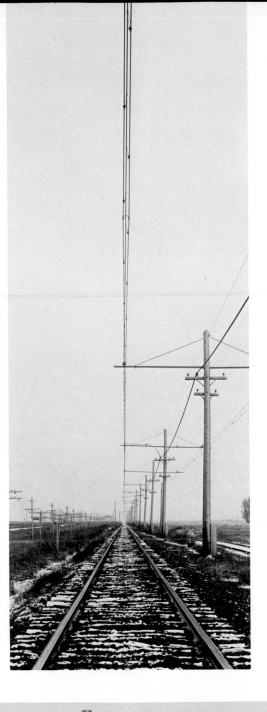

THE LONG WINTER

As gloomy as the future looked on October 31, 1973, the axe does not fall. The electrification is saved once again by events far from Deer Lodge or Avery. In this case, by concerns over the latest Arab-Israeli war. Fears of an intensified fuel shortage, combined with an early winter and heavy traffic from the opening of new gateways, influence management to retain the motors.

The winter of 1973-74 comes early and stays late in the mountains of Montana, bringing Little Joes back to the Avery-Deer Lodge district, as well as to the east end of the Rocky Mountain Division. The return of electric traction to the Bitterroots is best illustrated by this Ted Benson photograph of E76 and E73 leading train No. 263 into the mountain grade at Bryson's Dominion Creek trestle.

We call this period *The Long Winter*. It will be marked by the heavy utilization of Little Joes as headend helpers on lash-ups of brand new SD40-2 and GP40 diesel power.

(Below) In Deer Lodge, beneath a photo of the Milwaukee Road's most modern electric motive power, the chief dispatcher and his assistant work at revising their trainsheet. It is now a second-generation diesel railroad, but Little Joes are the extra power keeping traffic moving this winter.

All— Ted Benson

139

Ed Austin

140

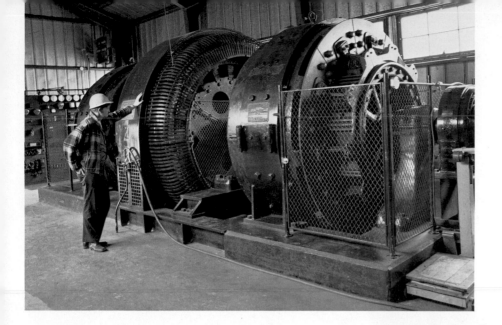

Janney substation, in the hills south of Butte, provides power for the Pipestone Pass grade, and contains regulator panels for the remote control operation of the substations at Morel, Gold Creek and Ravenna. As you visit here while the December snows are whipping around the red brick substation, the friendly operator invites you inside to view the electrical apparatus and the highly interesting control console. Then, because you're really lucky, he takes you in the back room to see the 3500-KVA transformer and 3000-KW motor-generator set purchased in 1955 by Laurence Wylie from the Cleveland Union Terminal. A similar set, purchased at the same time, went to Cle Elum substation on the Coast Division. The builder's plate cautions you to "read the instruction book" before operating!

Further up the grade, on May 21, 1974, Little Joes E70 and E79 lead a pair of diesels, and 134 cars weighing in at 5390 tons, toward Pipestone Pass tunnel.

Once I was riding over Butte Hill, when the diesels broke down on our eastbound train. It was a good day, with dry rail and no wind to blow the sand off the rails. We were right next to Janney substation, so I gave the engineer approval to go. Running at 475 amperes per traction motor, those Joes pulled the train over the hill with no trouble. I did some calculations later that showed that each of the locomotives had to produce 6700 to 7000 horsepower, at 30 percent adhesion, to pull that train. —T. Barry Kirk, former chief electrical engineer, as interviewed by Noel T. Holley.

Lightning, a very powerful enemy of the electrification, struck again in July 1973, just below Janney, ending the career of the E34 motors. The Janney substation operator tells Noel T. Holley how his station is uniquely "protected" from that hazard:

The motor-generator set we got from the Cleveland Union Terminal could put out as much power as all three Milwaukee motor-generators combined. It was really rugged, too. Lightning would sometimes strike the trolley and cause a flash-over inside the Milwaukee sets. The big one from the C.U.T. would just rumble through and keep right on going!

ARMAGEDDON AND CREATION

It must be the sight of the nearly full moon through the pan of the E77 that finally calms me down. It is a freezing, cold night in December 1973, at Avery, and we've been waiting since noon for train 2-262. The assignment had called for some photographs of the Joe on the steep mountain grade.

I am still furious about the delay, but seeing that moon helps cool me down. Maybe...just maybe...this will work out satisfactorily after all. Nobody shoots photographs at night from moving trains, but maybe it's possible. I quickly photograph motor No. E77 as the train arrives, and then step onto a trailing diesel unit.

Soon we are headed up into the Bitterroot Mountains, and as we slow to pick up the conductor, the first shot is from the nose of our SD40-2. Not bad, I think to myself, maybe this WILL work...

Taking advantage of our stop to pick up the conductor, I move up to the diesel unit immediately behind motor E77. As we start again, the view from the low-nose of the SD40-2 becomes increasingly wild and fast moving. Just below the North Fork bridge, a constant-lit green signal swims into view, leaving a shaky image on the film. The brightness of the moon has combined with the reflective surface of the snow, to give us an incredibly bright nocturnal landscape.

(Above) It is terribly cold upon the cab nose while traveling at 30 miles an hour, making hands and face immobile. Words begin to slur because of face muscles too cold to move. Just below Falcon, we begin to slow down and it is possible to get a picture looking down upon the E77 in the moonlight.

What luck! The pin connecting the Wylie diesel-controller with the Joe's throttle had fallen out in the darkness of the cab, leaving the engineer momentarily with just E77 to pull the train and idling diesels.

Picking up speed again, with the pin back in place, we enter the first of the tunnels and the 3400-volt arcing begins...

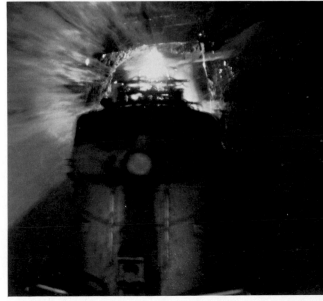

Russell B. Austin

From Adair onward, the climb up to St. Paul Pass becomes a frightening, yet exhilarating, experience. It is The Creation, and Armageddon, wrapped up into one...Fort Sumpter and Iwo Jima. Falling sparks, ice, and water, drop down on us from both pantographs.

The long tunnels are even worse, with all of the arcing and flashing enveloping us inside the bore.

Finally, we top the summit at the east end of the St. Paul Pass tunnel and the arcing slows down. Then the Joe starts regenerating down the grade with both pans sparking like giant strobe lights. The trees become a succession of stroboscopic images...a dizzying sight that lasts as far as Haugan. It must be a spectacular show from Interstate 90, for the drivers of the few cars and trucks on the road.

By the time we get to Alberton, the cold and the excitement have gotten to me. I alight at the station and look for a meal at the Silver Grill, before ducking into the little Montana Hotel across from the depot. I hit the bed like a ton of bricks.

Laying in bed, all I can think is...Wow! —Author

As winter wears on in the Deer Lodge Valley, Little Joes are still very much in evidence, hauling trains across a countryside where diesel oil and gasoline are still in short supply. At Deer Lodge roundhouse, there is a new kind of quiet respect for the electric locomotives. Men are conscious of the uniqueness of their jobs as they change out a traction motor, or engaged in the fiery work of changing a tire on motor E21. The "Men Who Know Electricity" sign takes on a new meaning, and the old twin-armature traction motor from a scrapped Westinghouse locomotive, a spare for rotary plow X900214, seems to be part of an incredibly distant past.

There is a cathedral-like hush at the Deer Lodge roundhouse, where workers stop to admire the bruised face of motor No. E77, the champion of innumerable winter nights in the Bitterroots and in the Rockies.

All— Ted Benson

(Above) It never happened, but what if the Milwaukee Road had electrified a branch line? A hint to the answer lies in this photograph, which shows the two-unit Harlowton switcher operating under the mile of trolley wire on the Great Falls branch adjacent to the yard. Scrapping of the wrecked E83, in 1952, left just three steeple-cab switchers, barely enough to protect the yards at Butte and Deer Lodge. This and the long trains handled at Harlowton helped assure that ES-3 boxcab switchers would be standard power in this yard. The motors today are the E57B and the E34C.

(Left) On an afternoon in May, Tom Buckley, electric locomotive engineer, starts his day by draining the air reservoirs on motor E57B, a carry-over from the long-gone days of steam.

*I ran one of those detour trains over
the BN once...the track was so darned
level that it almost made me feel sick
to my stomach.* —Engineer

Inside the crowded cab, Buckley starts his afternoon
switching job with the E57B and E34C units. We observe him
as he crosses both his arms to simultaneously control the
brakes and the throttle of the motors for a complex switching
move. The field man and switching conductor discuss the
day's yard duties; one an experienced electric railroader, the
other a young man whose future will involve diesel-electric
motive power.

Warren M. Marcus

The contrast between the mainstream of American railroad technology and the funky operations of the Milwaukee electrification in the 1970's is never sharper than in the spring of 1974. Here comes train No. 261, the *XL Special*, storming westward out of Butte underneath the ridge of the Continental Divide. On the point is a 25-year-old Little Joe, tightly coupled to a pair of brand new SD40-2's and General Motors' test locomotive No. 5740. This interesting lash-up is operating under a catenary strung 59 years earlier. The uncreosoted Idaho Red Cedar trolley poles were stubbed, instead of being replaced, more than 35 years ago. The train is proceeding along a rock-and-roll track structure toward Avery, where Jim Lowery presides over a substation with a very leaky roof, necessitating a huge plastic sheet to cover one of the m-g sets.

What can the General Motors technician, riding the SD45-X test locomotive, be thinking of this railroad operation?

In Avery, retired engineer Harold Theriault is our last living link with the earliest days of the electrification and the Pacific Extension. The good-looking youngster who helped the first surveyors that walked down out of the North Fork has finally grown old.

Sitting by his window overlooking Avery yard, Harold tells stories about the giants of the past...tales of the 1910 fire, when Johnny Mackedon became the hero of Avery, and about how Japanese sectionmen bravely faced the flames, never to return. The stories roll on, about Blundell and the wreck of No. 15, "Hooter" Drake and "Redboard" Murray...men whose spirits will always live in the shadows of the lonely canyons of the Bitterroots.

"Don't call those old GE motors Pelicans! They were the finest locomotives this electrification, and this railroad, ever saw!," admonishes Harold.

(Right) Unfortunately, it is very late in the day for the Milwaukee electrification, and the reprieve that keeps the Little Joes in operation does not extend to the boxcab motors of Harold's youth. At Deer Lodge, the E45 set stands derelict behind the roundhouse after its last assignment as the Butte Helper. Soon it will be on its way west for the last time, headed for the scrappers on the Coast.

Train No. 263, rolling over the hump at Groveland with 106 cars in its consist, is an excellent example of electric railroading in Eastern Montana in the spring of 1974. Just ahead of motors E76 and E73 is the 1.4 percent grade to Loweth, and then, when the summit is reached, the long descent to the Missouri River at Lombard.

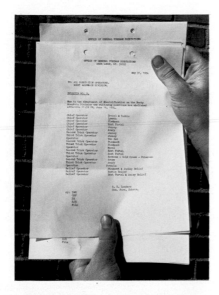

By June 1974, the old issue of the Gap, the new problems of lower traffic levels, combine with an easing of the gasoline shortage to bring about the demise of the electrics.

An announcement arrives at the end of May... notifying Milwaukee Road employees that June 16, 1974, will be the last day of electric operation on the Rocky Mountain Division. Additionally, many jobs will be permanently abolished.

(Bottom) The last set of Joes departed from Avery late in the morning of June 14, on the point of train No. 264. Now, in late afternoon, a lone employee is on duty at the enginehouse, which will never again be populated by live electrics. Nearby, one of the original trolley construction cars still survives to the end. By November, word will come down from headquarters that Avery is to be eliminated as a division point, in favor of St. Maries.

On June 14th the end of electric operations finally arrives for substation operator Don Goodsell at Avery. He witnessed the departure of the last electric train from his district several hours earlier, and is now awaiting the end of a favorite job and the start of a new career in electrical contracting. For legions of electric railway fans, it is the loss of a great and popular institution.

Alan Steinheimer

Train No. 264, which had left Avery on the last run, the day before, pulls past the old Missoula depot at dawn on June 15, 1974.

Little Joes E73 and E20, along with diesels 183, 189, and 17, arrive at Deer Lodge at 7:50 a.m. The crew poses with Division Superintendent Stan Jones for a formal portrait, depicting the end of mainline electrical operations. The final westbound electrically-operated No. 263 train, which operated the day before, was hauled by motors E79 and E71, leading diesels 3013, 3124, and 296. The motive power came in with only the head of its train, after several cars derailed east of town.

(Right) After the cameras have taken the last photos, engineer Bill Lintz walks into the roundhouse locker room to sign off duty at 9:10 a.m. By that routine action, Lintz ends a history of nearly 59 years of mainline electric operations, spanning a period that ranged from the development of the earliest aircraft to the exploration of our solar system. The young man who fired for "Hooter" Drake has become the last engineer of a mainline electric.

Roundhouse foreman Leo N. Kemp, and his assistant, get steeple-cab E82 ready for switching duties late on the night of June 15th. Bryan Gustafson, the young engineer from the Bitterroots helper job, will use the E82 to switch the Deer Lodge yard until 3:00 a.m. on the 16th, at which time he will take the engine back to the roundhouse and drop the pantograph to end the last operation of a Milwaukee electric locomotive.

(Below) W. H. Wilkerson, an engineer from the east end, captures the last photograph taken of the Harlowton switcher at work, just before it ties up at 11:40 p.m. on the night of June 15th.

The motor-generator sets are now quiet, and substation operators will remain only to act as watchmen until scrapping of the power distribution system can take place.

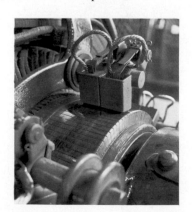

ARRIVALS — Chicago, Milwaukee, St. Paul and Pacific — ENGINE HOUSE REGISTER

DATE	TRAIN	ENGINE	TIME OF ARRIVAL in YARD	TIME CUT OFF TRAIN	TIME ON ENGINE TRACK	ENGINEMAN	MILEAGE TO DATE	FIREMAN	MILEAGE TO DATE	OFF DUTY BEFORE COMMENCING THIS TRIP Hours	Mins.	ON DUTY During 24 Hour Period Ending With This Trip Hours	Mins.	ENGINEMAN Time Released From Duty	Time Available For Further Service	ARRIVAL AND DEP. Time Released From Duty	Available For Further Service
6-14	262				12⁰⁰	Goldie	2684	—		24	—	1	05	12³⁵A	8³⁵A		
6-14	SW	E82				Gustafson				16	—	9	00	7A	12⁰⁰		
6-14 74	96					Hansen		—									
6-14 74	SW	E82				Jennings	2369			14	45	8	50	6⁵⁰P	2⁵⁰A		
6-15 74	262					Jones	3040										
6-15 74	SW	E82				Gustafson				15	—	8	—	3⁴⁰P			
6-15 74	264 +3	E73-20	7 50			Lintz				8	—	5 50		9¹⁄₂A	5¹⁰		
6-15 74	D.H.	Bus				Royston		—		—		5 00					
6-15 74	D.H.					WALKER		—		8	—	3²⁵A					
6-15 74	SW	E82				WALKER		—	—	8	—	8	—	6²⁰A	2 00		
6-16 74	SW	E82				Gustafson				16	—	8	—	3A	11⁴⁵		
6-16 74	202	186+2	4⁴⁵			Prairie	2416			24 20	3	55		5²⁵A	1P		
6-16 74	264	74+2	6⁷			Morris				9 55	5	45		7³⁵	3⁴⁵		
6-16 74	SW	296				WALKER		—		16	—	8	15	6⁵P	2¹⁵		
6-16 74	261		8 30			Goldie	2980			18 25	4	25		9⁰⁰P	5²⁵A		
6-17 74	SW	296				Gustafson				16	—	11	45	6⁷A	2P		
6-17 74	264 +4		5²⁵			Kingl	2038	—		13 40	7	35		6²⁰P	2³⁰A		
6-17 74	SW	296	9⁴⁵			Jennings	2549	—		24	—	10	—	10⁰⁰P	8³⁰A		

(Above) The roundhouse register for June 15-16 records the last entries of engineers Bill Lintz (line 7), and Bryan Gustafson (line 11).

(Below) The shut-down of electric operations has mandated that all electric locomotives, except No. E57B at Harlowton, be brought to Deer Lodge for the start of salvage operations. It is a very full round-house on the night of June 16, 1974. To the left of the post are the E73 and E20 motors from the last run. On the right is No. E79 from the last westbound run. None were prepared for a safe tomorrow.

The end has finally arrived.

POST-ELECTRIFICATION

When Bryan Gustafson dropped the pantograph of motor E82 from live trolley wire, he signaled the end of a way of life for hundreds of Rocky Mountain Division railroaders. Scrapping of the electrical system's 20 million pounds of copper began shortly thereafter, creating such scenes as that at Roland, where only the steel messenger wires remain after removal of the copper overhead.

For the "town" of Roland, at the west end of the St. Paul Pass tunnel, it is the stripping away of one of the last reminders of the past, just short of removal of the tracks themselves.

The ending of electrical operations is a blow to Laurence Wylie, retired genius of the electrification. Wylie will die in retirement at Seattle in 1978, after a long and happy life.

For Bill Brautigam, the retired master mechanic at Deer Lodge, and electric locomotive expert, it is a disappointment too. Brautigam, who died in Southern California in 1977, said if he were to design a modern electric railroad for the future, it would be an all alternating current system.

Laurence Wylie—
Genius of the electrification

Willard "Bill" Brautigam—
Locomotive expert

A. Bruce Butler

All Little Joes, except No. E70, go westward to the Coast for scrapping. We witness the end of the line for motor E76 on New Year's Eve 1974, at the Seattle Iron and Metal Company. Three of the Joes are dismantled here, while the remainder are sent to the Purdy Company scrapyard at Chehalis, Washington. The stripped forms of the E74 and E79 will survive outside the latter yard until 1978, when they, too, will be torched.

The Joes were built to lead easy lives on the state-owned railroads of the Soviet Union. But fate decreed that they make their home on one of the toughest mainlines in the West, on a railroad too poor even to convert all of their driving axles to roller bearings.

The end came in August 1974 for the most-photographed boxcab set, the E34 motors. Their careers ended in 1973 near Newcomb, when they were struck by lightning while helping a diesel freight train eastward on Pipestone Pass.

(Right) The electrification still lives in other ways, such as in the license plate of Montana railfan Arthur S. Jacobsen, shown with his "E50A" on the rails at Renton, Washington.

The smoke pouring from St. Paul Pass tunnel illustrates another of the effects of all-diesel operation of the Pacific Extension in 1974.

Noel T. Holley

163

The road sign on U.S. Highway 10 in St. Regis is one of the reminders of electric days on the Milwaukee Road. From Tacoma to Othello, Avery to Deer Lodge, and Deer Lodge to Harlowton, the trolley system is dead. By 1979, even the continued existence of the railroad itself will be in doubt.

(Below) Three classes of Milwaukee locomotives are still moving trains along the shores of Puget Sound, on the HO-scale model railroad of Keith and Dawn Newsom, where the Milwaukee electrification is fondly remembered.

Little Joe E70 is preserved in downtown Deer Lodge, not far from the mountains of its greatest exploits. For the E70, the former GE750 demonstrator, it is a well-deserved rest after 25 years of incredibly demanding service on a slowly deteriorating track structure.

Bipolar E2 found a home in St. Louis in the early 1960's, at the National Museum of Transport.

(Left) Also preserved is ES-3 switcher E57B, the Harlowton switcher. The repainted motor, less its E34C booster, is displayed in Harlowton at Chief Joseph Park, named for the famous leader of the Nez Perce Indian tribe.

(Below) The E50 set, the old 10200 motor, survives today in Duluth, Minnesota, at the Lake Superior Transportation Museum. The Milwaukee Road, and the world, owe a debt of gratitude to these motors, which proved the merits of regeneration and long-distance electrification for mainline railroads.

Milwaukee Road

BIBLIOGRAPHY

BOOKS

Brain, Insley J. Jr., *The Milwaukee Road Electrification,* San Mateo: The Western Railroader, 1961.

Derleth, August, *The Milwaukee Road: Its First Hundred Years*, New York: Creative Age Press, 1948.

Middleton, William D., *When The Steam Railroads Electrified*, Milwaukee: Kalmbach Publishing Company, 1974.

Scribbins, Jim, *The Hiawatha Story,* Milwaukee: Kalmbach Publishing Company, 1970.

Swett, Ira L., *Montana Trolleys III,* South Gate: Interurbans Magazine, 1970.

Wood, Charles R. and Dorothy M., *Milwaukee Road West,* Seattle: Superior Publishing Company, 1972.

Zimmerman, Karl R., *The Milwaukee Road Under Wire*, New York: Quadrant Press, 1973.

ARTICLES

Cummings, Doug E., Douglas, Ken L., and Will, Dick, "The Milwaukee Road Electrics" (roster), *Extra 2200 South*, January-February 1972.

Dellinger, E.S., "Trail of the Olympian," *Railroad Magazine,* July 1950.

Dietrich, Donald C., "The Story of the Milwaukee Electrification," *Railroad Magazine,* June 1970.

Middleton, William D., "Classics," *Trains Magazine,* July 1970.

Rogers, Gordon W., "Butte, Anaconda & Pacific," *Trains Magazine,* July 1963.

Warner, Paul T., "The Chicago, Milwaukee, St. Paul & Pacific Railroad," *Pacific Railway Journal,* . June 1958.

BROCHURES

The Electric Divisions of the Chicago, Milwaukee & St. Paul Railway, Schenectady: General Electric Company, 1925.

The Milwaukee Electrification - A Proud Era Passes, Chicago: The Milwaukee Road, 1973.

The King of the Rails, Chicago, Milwaukee & St. Paul Railway, Chicago, 1915.

The ghosts of Little Joes and the men who ran them will continue to haunt the high country of Montana, Idaho, and Washington, long after the men of this generation have passed away. People not yet born will someday learn that electric trains once operated here, and that something unique to the Pacific Northwest, and to America, is gone.

While we were rebuilding the No. 4449 **Daylight** *engine, we needed some grab irons for the steps in front. Somebody showed up with a couple, from the derelict E79. So when you see the No. 4449 steaming past some day, you are also seeing parts of a Little Joe.*
—A. Bruce Butler

3031
3031